TOP SECRET

TOP SECRET:

The Details of the Planned World War-II Invasion of Japan and

The Japanese Atomic Bomb!

How the Japanese Would Have Met It

–Documentary–

James Martin Davis and Bert Webber

WEBB RESEARCH GROUP PUBLISHERS

Please direct all inquiries to:
WEBB RESEARCH GROUP - PUBLISHERS
P.O. Box 314   Medford, OR 97501

We acknowledge the cooperation and permission of James Martin
Davis in allowing us to include material from his privately published
booklet *TOP SECRET; The Story of the Invasion of Japan* © 1985

Library of Congress Cataloging in Publication Data:

Davis, James Martin
        Top secret : the details of the planned World War II invasion of Japan
and how the Japanese would have met it : documentary / James Martin
Davis and Bert Webber
        p.   cm.
        Includes biographical references and index
        Strategy.48
        ISBN 0-936738-85-5
        1. World War, 1939-1945–Campaigns–Japan. 2. World War, 1939-
1945–United States. I. Webber, Bert. II. Title
        D767.2.037   1994   94-44934
        940.54'25–dc20   CIP

Contents

TBF "Avenger" patrols above invasion of Leyte. The number
of landing craft in event of invasion of Japan would have been
100-times greater.   —U.S. Navy

"Operation Downfall"

Deep in the recesses of the National Archives in Washington, D. C., hidden for over four decades, lie thousands of pages of yellowing and dusty documents. These documents, which are now declassified, still bear the stamp

"TOP SECRET"

Contained in these little examined documents are the detailed plans for "Operation Downfall." This was the code name for the scheduled American invasion of Japan.

Only a few Americans in 1945, and fewer Americans today, are aware of the elaborate plans that had been prepared for the American invasion of the Japanese home islands. Even fewer are aware of how close America actually came to launching that invasion and of what the Japanese had in store for the Americans had the invasion of Japan actually been started.

"Operation Downfall" was prepared in its final form during the spring and summer of 1945. This plan called for two massive military undertakings to be carried out in succession, and aimed at the very heart of the Japanese Empire.

In the first invasion, in what was code named "Operation Olympic," American combat troops would be landed by amphibious assault during the early morning hours of November 1, 1945 on Japan itself. After an unprecedented naval and aerial bombard-ment, 14 combat divisions of American soldiers and marines would land on heavily fortified and defended Kyushu, the southernmost of the Japanese home islands.

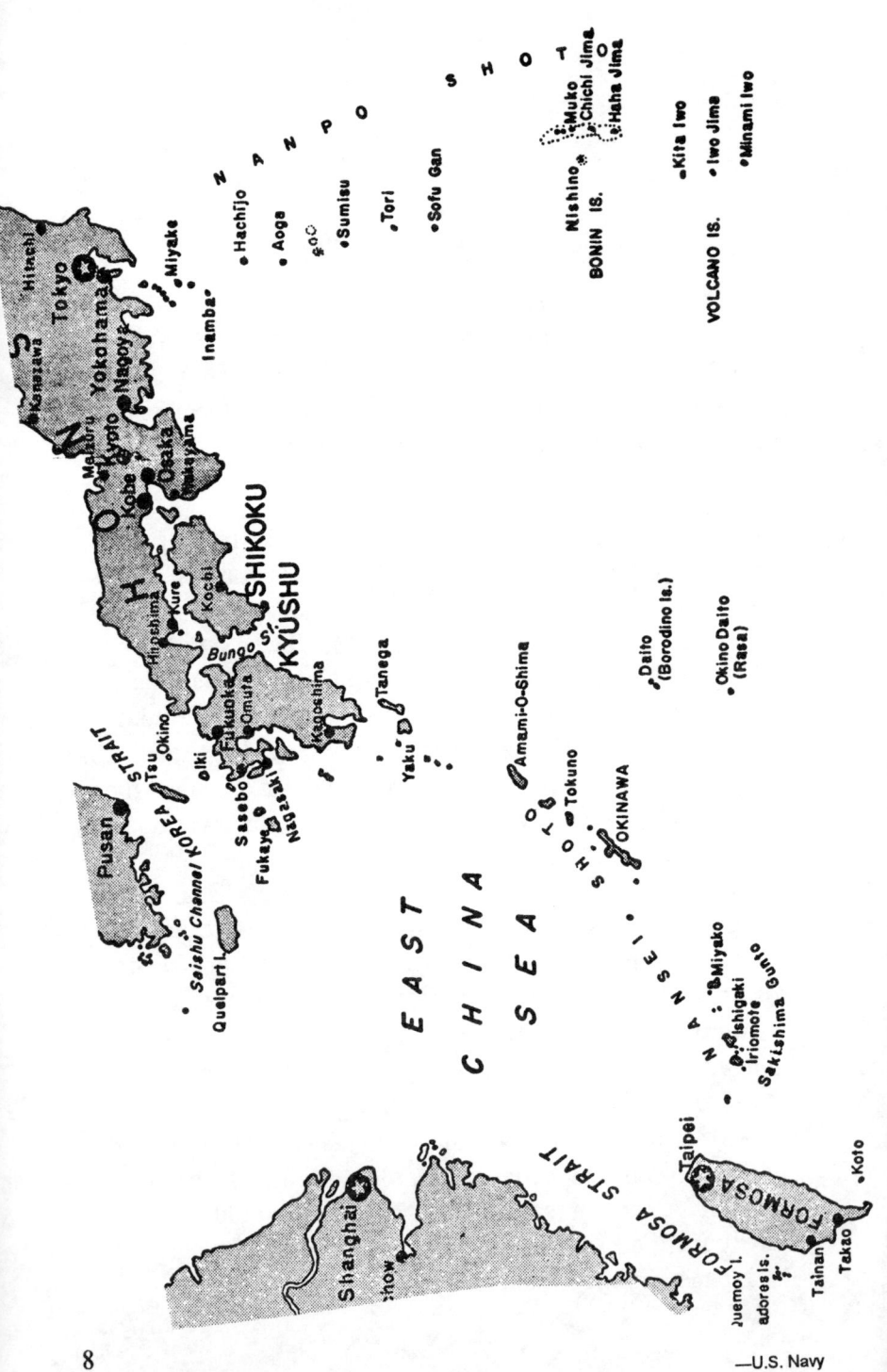

8

—U.S. Navy

On March 1, 1946, the second invasion, code named "Operation Coronet," would send at least 22 more American combat divisions against one million Japanese defenders to assault the main island of Honshu and the Tokyo (Kanto) Plain. This would be in a final effort to obtain the unconditional surrender of Japan.

With the exception of a part of the British Pacific Fleet, "Operation Downfall" was to be a strictly American operation. It called for the utilization of the entire United States Marine Corps, the employment of the entire United States Navy in the Pacific, and for the efforts of the 7th Air Force, the 8th Air Force recently deployed from Europe, the 20th Air Force, and for the American Far Eastern Air Force. Over 1.5 million combat soldiers, with millions more in support, would be directly involved in these two amphibious assaults.

> A total of 4.5 million American servicemen – over 40 percent of all servicemen still in uniform in 1945 – were to be a part of "Operation Downfall."

The invasion of Japan was to be no easy military undertaking. Casualties were expected to be extremely heavy. Admiral William Leahy estimated that there would be over 250,000 Americans killed or wounded on Kyushu alone. General Charles Willoughby, General Douglas MacArthur's Chief of Intelligence, estimated that American casualties from the entire operation would be one million men by the fall of 1946. General Willoughby's own intelligence staff considered this to be a conservative estimate.

During the summer of 1945, America had little time to prepare for such a monumental endeavor, but the top military leaders were in almost unanimous agreement that such an invasion was a necessity.

While a naval blockade and strategic bombing of Japan

Otomari

La Perouse Strait

HOKKAIDO
Sapporo
Muroran
Hakodate
Strait
Ominato
Tsugaru
Hachinohe

Vladivostok

SEA OF
JAPAN

Sendai
Sado
Niigata

Utsuryo

Oki
Kanazawa
Hitachi

Tokyo
Maizuru
Kyoto
Yokohama
Taegu
Kobe
Nagoya
Pusan

Osaka
Tsu
Okino
Hiroshima
Wakayama
Miyake

Kure
Iki
Kochi
Inamba

Sasebo
Fukuoka
Omuta
Hachijo

Nagasaki
SHIKOKU
Aoga

KYUSHU
Kagoshima
Sumisu

Tanega
Tori

Yaku
Sofu Gan

KOREA STRAIT

Bungo S.

HONSHU

NANPO

SHOTO

Amami-O-Shima

Nishino
Muko
Chichi Jima
BONIN IS.
Haha Jima

—U.S. Navy

was considered to be useful, General MacArthur considered a naval blockade of Japan ineffective to bring about an unconditional surrender. General George C. Marshall was of the opinion that air power over Japan, as it was over Germany, would not be sufficient to bring an end to the war. While most of the American top military minds believed that a continued naval blockade and the strategic bombing campaign would further weaken Japan, few of them believed that the blockade or the bombing would bring about an unconditional surrender.

The advocates for invasion agreed that while a naval blockade chokes, it does not kill. Strategic bombing might destroy cities but it still leaves whole enemy armies intact. Both General Eisenhower and General Ira C. Eaker, the Deputy Commander of the Army Air Force agreed. Therefore, on May 25, 1945, the Combined Chiefs of Staff, after extensive deliberation, issued to General Douglas MacArthur, to Admiral Chester Nimitz, and to Air Force's General "Hap" Arnold, the "TOP SECRET" directive to proceed with the invasion of Kyushu. The target date was set – for obvious reasons after the typhoon season – for November 1, 1945.*

On July 24th, President Harry Truman approved the report of the Combined Chiefs of Staff, which called for the initiation of Operations "Olympic" and "Coronet." On July 26th, the United Nations issued the Potsdam Proclamation. This called upon Japan to surrender unconditionally or face "total destruction." Three days later, on July 29th, DOMEI, the Japanese government news agency, broadcast to the world that Japan would ignore the proclamation of Potsdam and would refuse to surrender. This action by the Japanese,

---

* Although the war was over, as a direct result of the successful atomic bombing of Hiroshima and Nagasaki in August, and no invasion of Japan would have to be undertaken, when the typhoon of October 8, 1945, hit, it devastated American ships and ruined stockpiles of foodstuffs and munitions at Okinawa, the planned staging area for the invasion of Japan.

therefore sealed the invasion plans.

During this same time period, the intelligence section of the Federal Communications Commission monitored internal Japanese radio broadcasts, which disclosed that Japan had taken specific actions in the face of what some called the coming invasion of the home islands:

The government closed all the schools to mobilize its school-age children

It was arming its civilian population

It was forming the people into national civilian defense units,

The Japanese government was turning the country into a nation of fortified caves and underground defenses in preparation for the expected invasion of their homeland.

The cover on the *TOP SECRET* document for "Operation Downfall"
—J. M. Davis

Operation "Olympic"

"Operation Olympic," the invasion of Kyushu, would come first. "Olympic" called for a four-pronged assault from the sea on Kyushu. Its purpose was

> To seize and control the southern third of that island and to establish American naval and air bases there in order to effectively intensify the bombings of Japanese industry
>
> To tighten the American and British naval blockade of the home islands
>
> To destroy units of the main Japanese army
>
> To support Operation "Coronet," the scheduled invasion of the Tokyo Plain that was to come the following March.

On October 27th, the preliminary invasion would begin

KYUSHU

—Japan National Tourist Organization

when the 40th Infantry Division would land on a series of small islands to the west and southwest of Kyushu. At the same time, the 158th Regimental Combat Team would invade and occupy a small is-land (Tanegashima – TANEGA IS.) 28 miles to the south of Kyushu. On these islands, seaplane bases would be established and radar would be set up to provide advance air warning for the invasion fleet, to serve as fighter direction centers for the carrier based aircraft and to provide an emergency anchorage for the invasion fleet, should things not go well on the day of the invasion.

As the invasion grew imminent, the massive power of the United States Navy would approach Japan. The naval forces scheduled to take part in the actual invasion consisted of two awesome fleets – the U. S. Third and the Fifth.

The Third Fleet, under Admiral William F. "Bull" Halsey, with its 16-inch guns and carrier aircraft, would provide strategic support for the operation by targeting Honshu and Hokkaido in order to impede the movement of Japanese reinforcements south to Kyushu. The Third Fleet would be composed of a powerful group of battleships, heavy cruisers, destroyers and dozens of support ships. These, in addition to three fast carrier task groups. From the flat tops, hundreds of Navy fighters as well as dive bombers and torpedo planes would hit targets all over the island of Honshu.

The Fifth Fleet, under Admiral Raymond A. Spruance, would carry the invasion troops. This Fleet would consist of almost 3,000 ships including fast carriers and escort carrier task forces. These fighting ships would provide gunfire and be the covering force with bombardment and fire support for a joint expeditionary force. This landing flotilla would include thous-ands of additional landing craft of all types and sizes.

Several days before the invasion, the battleships, heavy cru-isers and destroyers would pour thousands of tons of

Invasion Beach Code Names

The names of the 31 invasion beaches of Japan were a recital of automobile brand names:

Austin
Buick
Cadillac
Chevrolet
Chrysler
Cord
DeSoto
Dusenberg
Essex
Ford
Franklin
Hupmobile
Locomobile
Lincoln
LaSalle
Moon
Mercedes
Maxwell
Overland
Oldsmobile
Packard
Plymouth
Pontiac
Reo
Rolls Royce
Saxon
Star
Studebaker
Stutz
Winston
Zephyr

high explosives into the target areas. They would not cease the bomb-ardment until after the invasion had been launched.

The invasion was planned for the early morning hours of November 1, 1945. Thousands of American soldiers and marines would pour ashore on beaches all along the eastern, southeastern, southern and western coasts of Kyushu.

The Eastern Assault Force, consisting of the 25th, 33rd and the 41st Infantry Divisions, would land near Miyasaki, at beaches called Austin, Buick, Cadillac, Chevrolet, Chrysler and Cord. They would move inland to attempt to capture Miyasaki and its nearby airfield.

The Southern Force, made up on the 1st Cavalry Division, the 43rd Division and Americal Division would land inside Ariake Bay at beaches labeled DeSoto, Dusenberg, Essex, Ford and Franklin. The mission here would be the attempt to capture Shibushi and to take, further inland, the city of Kanoya and its surrounding airfields.

On the western shore of Kyushu, at beaches Pontiac, Reo, Rolls Royce, Saxon, Star, Studebaker, Stutz, Winston and Zephyr, the V Amphibious Corps would land the 2nd, 3rd and 5th Marine Divisions, sending half of its force inland to Sendai and the other half to the port city of Kagoshima.

On November 4th, (D+4) the reserve force, consisting of the 81st and 98th Infantry Divisions, and the 11th Airborne Divi-sion, after feigning an attack off the island of Shikoku, would be landed, if not needed elsewhere, near Kaimondake, which is on the southern-most tip of Kagoshima Bay, at beaches designated Locomobile, Lincoln, LaSalle, Hupmobile, Moon, Mercedes, Maxwell, Overland, Oldsmobile, Packard and Plymouth.

The objective of "Olympic" was to seize and control the island of Kyushu in order to use it for the launching plat-form for "Coronet." Operation "Coronet" was planned to be a final knock-out blow aimed at Tokyo and the Kanto Plain.

"Olympic" was not just a plan for invasion, but for conquest and occupation as well. It was expected to take four months to achieve its objectives, with three fresh American Divisions per month to be landed in support of that operation if needed. These additional troops would be taken from the units already assembling for "Coronet."

Troops of the 91st Infantry Division march in Memorial Day parade in Medford, Oregon having finished combat training at nearby Camp White. They soon landed at the Anzio beachhead in Italy, suffered heavy casualties. The 91st was destined to invade Japan as part of Operation "Coronet." See comments by Colonel Chris Hald, 361st Infantry Regt. on pages 66, 67.

Operation "Coronet"

If all went well with "Olympic," Operation "Coronet" would be launched on March 1, 1946. "Coronet" would be twice the size of "Olympic" with as many as 28 American Divisions to be landed on Honshu, the main Japanese island.

On March 1, 1946, all along the Chiba and Ibaraki Prefecture's coast east of Tokyo, the American 1st Army would land the 5th, 7th, 27th, 44th, 86th and 96th Infantry Divisions along with 1st, 4th and 6th Marine Divisions.

At Sagami Bay, just south of Tokyo, the entire 8th and 10th Armies would strike north and east to clear the long western shore of Tokyo Bay, and attempt to go as far as Yokohama.

The assault troops, landing to the south of Tokyo would be the 4th, 6th, 8th, 24th, 31st, 32nd, 37th, 38th and 87th Infantry Divisions, along with the 13th and 20th Armored Divisions.

Following the initial assault, eight more Divisions – the 2nd, 28th, 35th, 91st, 95th, 97th and 104th Infantry Divisions and the 11th Airborne Division – would be landed. If additional troops were needed, as expected they would be, other Divisions redeployed from Europe, undergoing training in the United States, would be shipped to Japan in what was hoped to be the final push. If the issue was critical and the troops in the U. S. had to be moved quickly, efficient and fast transport would have to be organized.

> **The key to victory in Japan rested with the success of "Olympic" at Kyushu. Without the success of the Kyushu campaign, "Coronet" might never be launched. The key to victory in Kyushu rested with American firepower, much of which was to be delivered by carrier launched aircraft.**

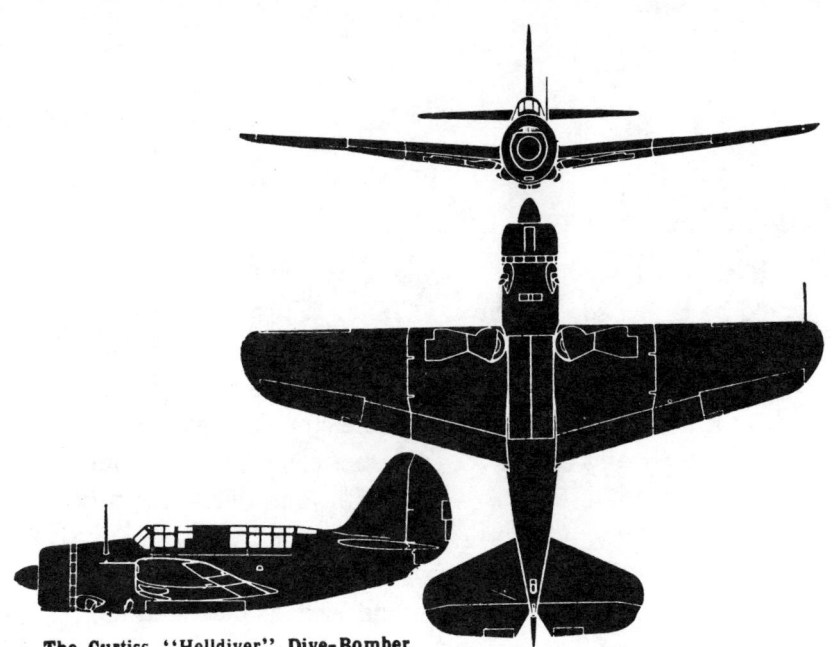

The Curtiss "Helldiver" Dive-Bomber.

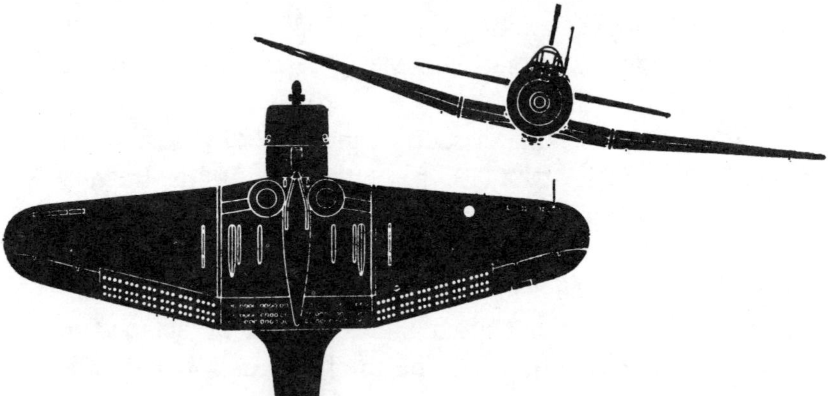

Aircraft silhouettes are from Jane's

The Douglas "Dauntless" Dive-Bomber.

At the outset of the invasion of Kyushu, waves of SBC Helldivers, SBD Dauntless dive bombers, TBF Avengers, F4U Corairs and F6F Hellcats would take off to bomb, rocket and strafe enemy defenses, gun emplacements and troop concentrations along the beaches. In all, there would be 66 aircraft carriers loaded with 2,649 naval and marine aircraft to be used for close-in air support while the soldiers were hitting the beaches.

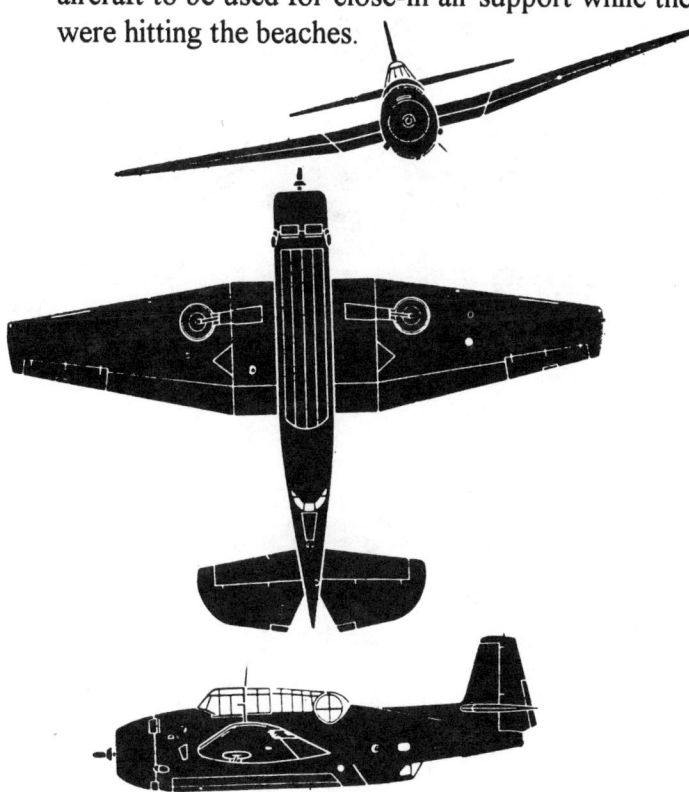

The Grumman "Avenger" Torpedo-Bomber.

These planes were also the fleet's primary protection against Japanese attack from the air. Had "Olympic" begun, these planes would be needed to provide an umbrella of protection for the soldiers and sailors of the invasion. Captured Japanese documents, and post-war interrogation

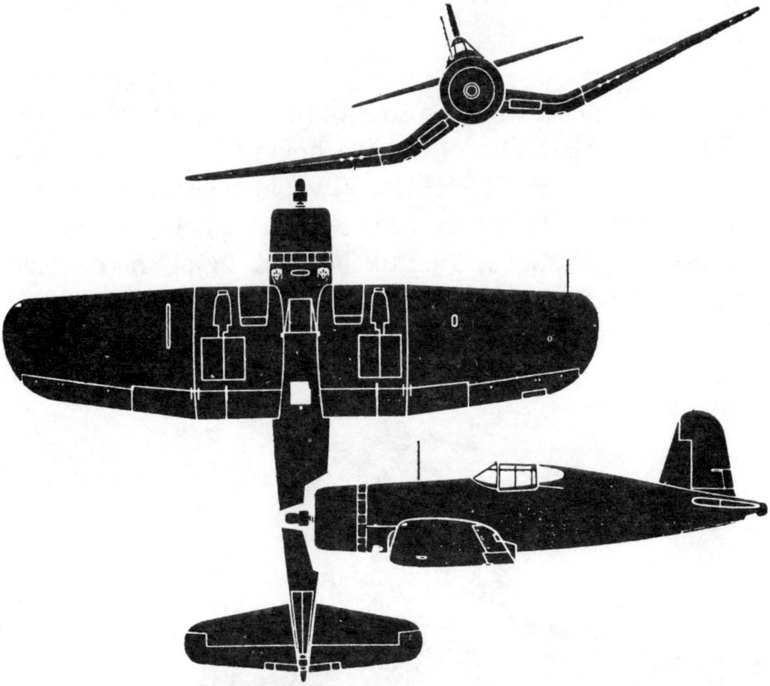

The Vought F4U-1 "Corsair" Single-seat Fighter.

The Grumman "Hellcat" Single-seat Fighter.

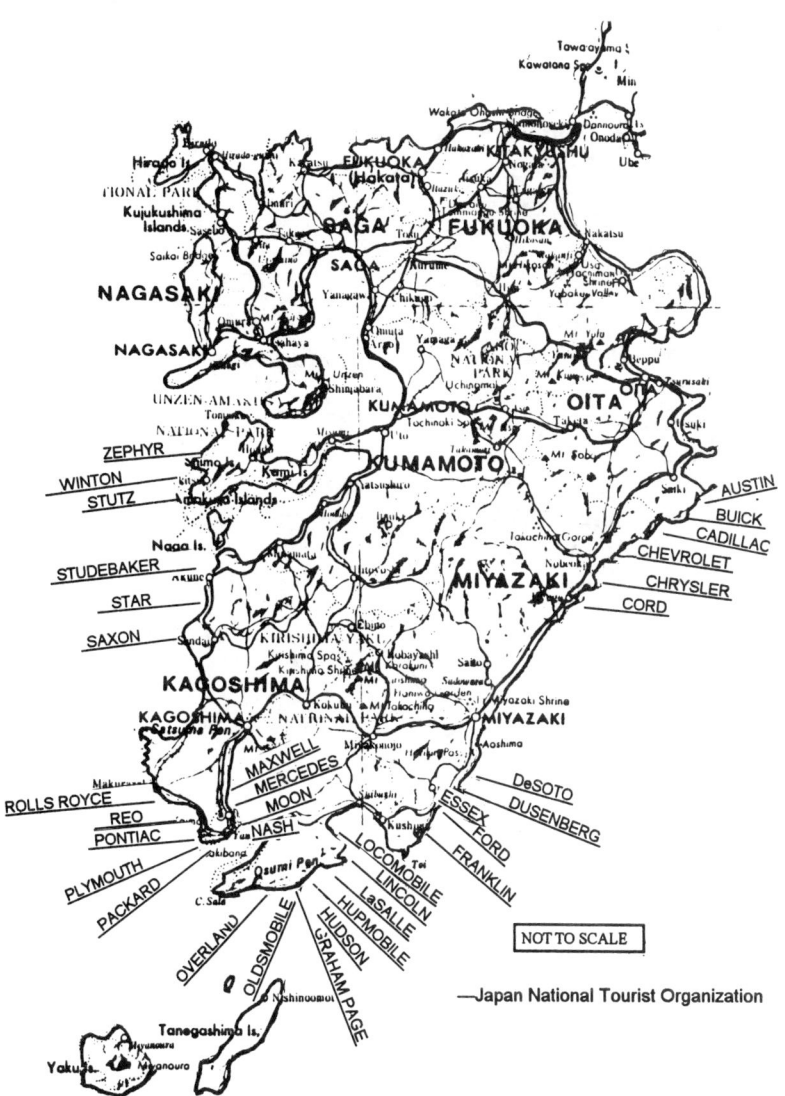

— Japan National Tourist Organization

NOT TO SCALE

PLANNED INVASION BEACHES OF KYUSHU

of Japanese military leaders,* disclose that our intelligence concerning the number of Japanese planes available for the defense of the home islands was dangerously in error. Severely low.

How Many Japanese Aircraft?

Allied intelligence had decided that the Japanese had no more than 2,500 aircraft of which they guessed only 300 would be deployed in suicide attacks. However, in August of 1945, undiscovered by U. S. intelligence, the Japanese still had 5,651 Army and 7,074 Navy aircraft, a total of 12,725 planes of all types.

---

* The *U. S. Strategic Bombing Survey* (USSBS) is made up of over 100 personal interviews of former Japanese officers conducted by American Naval officers immediately after the war when memories of the conquered were supposed to be still sharp. Now, years later, current researchers are advised to be aware that some things the former enemy revealed fail to hold up under scrutiny. A single example will illustrate the point: General Masatake Okumiya, who was in the Imperial Navy during the war, told the editor in 1975 that it "must be some mistake in translation [in 1945]" where he declared to then Captain, later Admiral James S. Russell, that the Japanese submarine *I-26* had launched an observation plane and spied on Seattle and the Puget Sound Naval Shipyard at Bremerton in June 1942. On hearing this, the very indignant *I-26* commander, Minoru Hasegaya declared to the editor: "My *I-26* never carried any aircraft during the Pacific War." Refer to *Silent Siege-III* in bibliography.

The Japanese Defense

Operation "Kits-Go"

> The Japanese Called
> The Plan For Their Final
> Defense
> "Kits-Go"

In the last months of the war, American military leaders were deathly afraid of the Japanese "Kamikaze" (The Divine Wind) and with good cause. These were usually Japanese fighter-type air-planes that were overloaded with bombs and piloted by mostly young flyers, often only semi-trained, for the specific purpose of diving the airplanes into an American capital ship and sinking it. The first instance of Kamikaze was the sinking of the CVE *St. Lo* on October 24, 1944 in the Philippine Sea near Leyte.

During the Okinawa campaign alone, Kamikaze aircraft sank over 30 ships and damaged over 400 others. During the summer months, American top brass had concluded that the Japs had spent their air force since American bombers and fighters flew un-molested over the shores of Japan on a daily basis.

What these military leaders did not know, was that by the end of July 1945, as part of the Japanese overall plan for the defense of their country, the Japanese had been saving many aircraft, much fuel and pilots in reserve, and had been feverishly building new planes for the decisive battle for their homeland. The Japs had abandoned, for the time, their suicide attacks in order to pre-serve their pilots and planes to hurl at American invasion fleets.

Airplanes commonly used for Kamikaze missions (top to bottom): Fighter 97Ki-27; Hayabusa Ki-43; Kawasaki Ki-61; 3 Hien Ki-61. Not shown is "Zero" ("Zeke") fighter. In last-defense posture, all Japanese aircraft would be used. — Orita

A large part of "Kits-Go" called for the use of the Japanese Naval and Air Forces in defense. Japan had been divided into districts. In each of these districts, hidden airfields were being built and hangers and aircraft were being dispersed and camo-uflaged in great numbers. Units were being trained. deployed and given final instructions. Still other suicide units were being scattered throughout the islands of Kyushu and elsewhere, and held in reserve, and for the first time in the war, the Army and Navy Air Forces would be operating under one single unified command.

As part of the "Kits-Go," the Japanese were building 20 suicide take-off strips in southern Kyushu with underground hangers for an all-out offensive. In Kyushu alone, the Japanese had 35 camouflaged airfield and 9 seaplane bases. As part of their overall plan, the seaplanes from these locations were also to be used in suicide missions.

On the night before the invasion, 50 seaplane bombers, along with 100 former carrier aircraft, and 50 land based army planes, were to be launched in a direct suicide attack on the American fleet.

The Japanese 5th Naval Air Fleet, and the 6th Air Army Force, had 58 more airfields on Korea, Western Honshu and Shikoku, which also were to be used for launching massive suicide attacks.

During July alone, 1,131 new planes were built and almost 100 new underground aircraft plants were in various stages of construction.

Every village had some type of aircraft manufacturing activity. Hidden in mines, railway tunnels, under viaducts and in basements of department stores, work was being done to construct new planes.

Additionally, the Japanese were building newer and more effective models of the "Ohka" ("Baka" bomber). This was a rocket propelled 2,640 pound bomb, much like the German V-1, but piloted to its final destination by a suicide

27

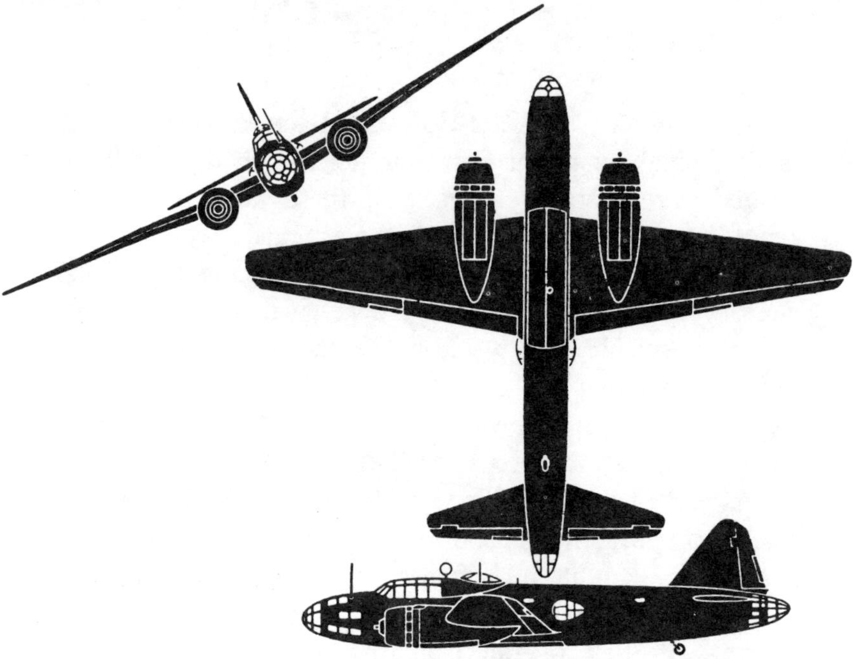

The Navy 1 Torpedo-Bomber ''Betty.''

"Betty" bomber carried Ohka steerable rocket bomb aloft, dropped it near target. Ohka also known as "Baka" (stupid) bomb.　　　　　　　　　　　　　　　　　　—Inoguchi

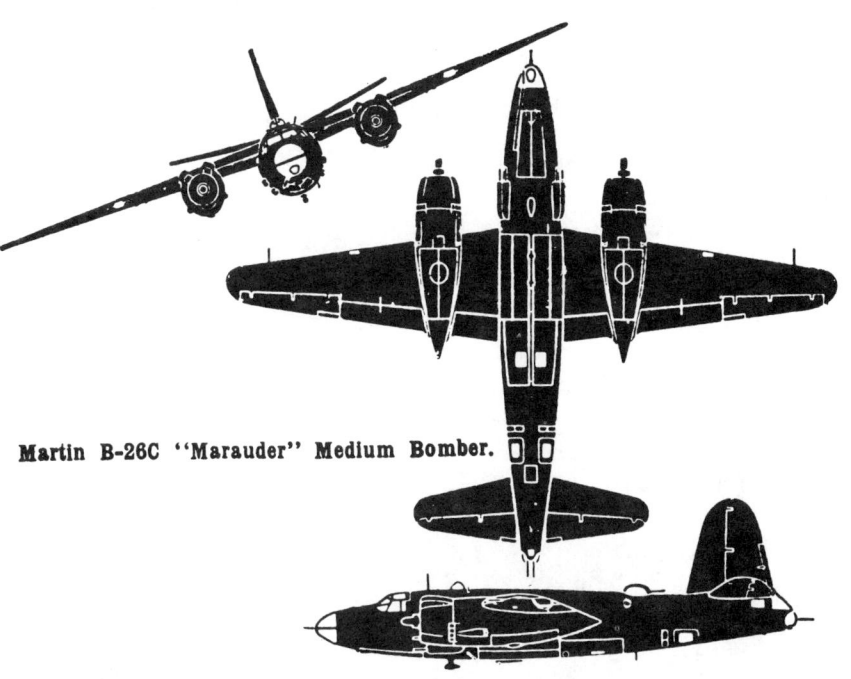

Martin B-26C "Marauder" Medium Bomber.

Although there are distinctive differences between the Japanese "Betty" (page 28) and the American B-26 (above), at a glance they had similiar looks – could be mis-identified in the air.

pilot after having been dropped from the under-belly of a "Betty" (twin-engine) bomber at about 27,000 feet altitude. The bomb would glide for a distance, then was supposed to "rocket" to the target.

In March of 1945, the Japanese had ordered about 800 of the earlier models of the "Ohka" to be built. By the summer of 1945, the Japanese were building a newer model which was to be catapulted out of caves in Kyushu to be used against the invasion ships which would be only minutes away. The "Ohka" had a level flight speed of 535 miles per hour. The Japanese called it their *Janrai-Butai* – "Divine Thunderbolt." *

* The first mission of several dozen "Ohkas," on March 21, 1945, near Okinawa, resulted in only 3 sinking any ships. The others were jettisoned by their mother planes so the "Bettys" could avoid American fighters. Then the "stupid" bombs, as the American sailors called the "Ohkas," were either shot down or, with nowhere to go, simply crashed into the sea.

An Ohka Experience

"Stand by to release *Ohka*.
"The targets are battleships."

The *Betty* twin-engine Mitsubishi bomber was cruising at 20,000 feet altitude. The *Ohka* pilot had been napping on a cot in the empty bomb bay for the last hour and was summoned to get ready for his duty.

The *Ohka* pilot shook hands with the *Betty's* commander then let himself down through the bomb bay door into the cockpit of his rocket bomb. There was a *gosport* (speaking tube) so the aircraft commander could give any final instructions.

A ship, believed to be an American battleship, was selected as the target. The mother airplane continued to fly toward it to minimize the distance the *Ohka* would have to glide into it. At about 18,000 feet altitude, and about five miles away from it, the commander yelled into the speaking tube that the rocket was being cut loose. The crew felt the airplane jolt upward as the rocket bomb broke away, then they peered out the small windows to watch it gliding below.

Quickly the falling missile grew smaller as it distanced itself from the bomber. All sight was lost as the airplane commander banked his craft in a steep 180-degree turn to leave the area as quickly as possible as flack from the ships was reaching for him. On this day, of 8 mother planes on *Ohka* runs, 6 had been shot down after releasing their charges and only 1 returned to the base.

As there was no radio communication between the bomber and the *Ohka,* no words could be exchanged and there would be no news of the rocket-pilot's last minutes. Hopefully the crew might see a gigantic explosion rising from below.

As the days passed, Kamikaze pilots were expended and replaced by others. As more days passed, these in turn were replaced by still newer ones. And so it went.

"The cherry blossoms had fallen but the trees were fresh and green." —based on Natasuka. See bibliography

The Army 8 Single-seat Fighter "Tony."

Experience with Kamikaze Sorties:

<u>Philippine campaign:</u>

421 flights; 43 returned; 388 expended with mixed results: 37 ships claimed sunk; 16 sunk; 68 claimed damaged; 87 damaged.

<u>Okinawa campaign:</u>

1,809 flights; 879 returned; 930 expended with mixed results: 44 ships claimed sunk; 17 ships sunk; 99 ships claimed damaged; 1,298 damaged.

Data known to be incomplete and often contrary.

Total claimed sunk: 276. Verified sinkings: 322.

Examples of known sunk included: 3 CVE; 13 DD, 5 LST, 3 APD.

Verified damages to 16 CV; 3, CVL; 17 CVE; 15 BB; 5 CA; 10 CL; 87 DD; 14 APA; 15 APD; 11 LST; 1 AH

CV Fleet carrier. CVE Escort carrier. CL Light cruiser. DD Destroyer.
BB Battleship. CA Heavy cruiser. APA Attack transport.
APD High speed transport. LST Landing ship, tank. AH Hospital ship

—Source: See bibliography for Inoguchi.

At Okinawa, while thousands of American sailors were wounded or had died as a result of kamikaze attacks, the kamikaze there had only limited success, primarily because of distance. Okinawa was located 350 miles from Kyushu and even experienced pilots flying from Japan became lost, ran out of fuel or did not have sufficient flying time to pick out a suitable target. Furthermore, early in the Okinawa campaign, the Americans had established a land based fighter command which, together with the carrier aircraft, provided an effective umbrella of protection against Kamikaze attacks.

During "Olympic," the situation would be reversed. Kamikaze pilots would have little distance to travel, would have considerable staying time over the invasion fleet, and would have little difficulty picking out suitable targets. Conversely, the American land based aircraft would be able to provide only minimal protection against suicide attacks since these American aircraft would have little flying time over Japan before they would be forced to return to their bases on Okinawa and elsewhere to refuel

Also different from the American invasion of Okinawa, would be the Japanese choice of targets. At Okinawa aircraft carriers and destroyers were the principal targets of the Kamikaze.

AMERICAN TROOPSHIPS, TARGETS

The Japanese targets for the "Olympic" invasion were to be the transports carrying the American troops who were to participate in the landings. The Japanese be-lieved they could kill far more Americans by sinking one troop ship than they could by sinking 30 destroyers.

The Japanese aim was to kill thousands of American troops at sea, thereby removing them from the actual landing. "Kits-Go" planners called for the destruction of 700 to 800 American ships.

When invasion became imminent, there would be a four-fold aerial plan of attack. While American ships were approaching Japan, but still in the open seas, an initial force of 2,000 army and navy fighters were to fight to the death in order to control the skies over Kyushu. A second force of 330, specially trained navy combat pilots, were to take off and attack the main body of the task force to keep it from using its fire support and air cover to adequately protect the troop carrying transports.

While these two forces were engaged, a third force of 825 suicide planes was to hit the American transports in the open seas.

As the convoys approached their anchorages, another 2,000 suicide planes were to be detailed in waves of 200 to 300, to be used in hour-by-hour attacks that would make Okinawa seem tame in comparison.

Letters From Some Kamikaze Pilots

I shall die watching the pathetic struggle of our nation.
> Like cherry blossoms
>> In the spring
> Let us fall
>> Clean and radiant
>> Ens. H. Okabe

Without regard for life or name, a Samurai will defend his homeland.
> Capt. T. Inogugchi

I think of springtime in Japan while soaring to dash against the enemy
> Lt. N. Ishibashi

Even though a thousand men fall to my right, and ten thousand to by left, I am going to score a direct hit on an enemy ship without fail.
> Ens. I. Hayashi

American troops would be arriving in approximately 180 lightly armed transports and 70 cargo vessels. Given the num-ber of Japanese planes and the short distance to target, certainly a large number of the American troop carrying trans-ports would have been hit.

By mid-morning of the first day of the invasion, due to limited fuel supply aboard most of the American land-based aircraft, these would be forced to return to their bases in Okinawa. The abandonment of the skies by the Americans would leave the defense against the suicide planes to the carrier pilots and the shipboard gunners. Initially, these pilots and gunners would have met with considerable success, but after the third, fourth and fifth waves of Japanese aircraft, a significant number of kamikaze most certainly would have broken through.

Carrier pilots, crippled by fatigue, would have to land time and time again to rearm and refuel – providing that their carriers had not been sunk or their landing decks "out of service" due to crashed kamikazes. Fighter planes do break down in the heat of battle. Where could a slightly damaged plane, or one that needed a quick tune-up, be parked on a heaving and possibly burning carrier deck to be fixed?

Guns do malfunction on both aircraft and combat vessels from the heat of continuous firing. Ammunition expended in such huge amounts would become scarce. Although gun crews would be exhausted by nightfall, the waves of Kamikazes would continue. With our fleet hovering off the beaches, all remaining Japanese aircraft would be committed to nonstop mass suicide attacks, which the Japanese hoped could be sustained for ten days.

The Japanese planned to coordinate their Kamikaze and conventional air strikes with attacks from the 40 remaining traditional submarines from the Imperial Japanese Navy. These attacks would begin when the invasion fleet was 180 miles off Kyushu. As the American invasion armada grew nearer, the rate of submarine attacks would increase. In addition to these sorties by the fleet submarines, some of which were to be armed with "Long Lance" torpedoes with a range of 20 miles, the Japanese had more frightening plans for death from the sea.

By the end of the war, the Japanese Navy still had 23 destroyers and two cruisers that were operational. These ships were to be used to counterattack the American invasion. A number of the destroyers were to be beached along the invasion beaches at the last minute to be used as anti-invasion gun platforms.

As early as 1944, Japan had established a special naval attack unit, which was the counterpart of the special attack units of the air force to be used in the defense of the homeland. These units were to be saved for the invasion and

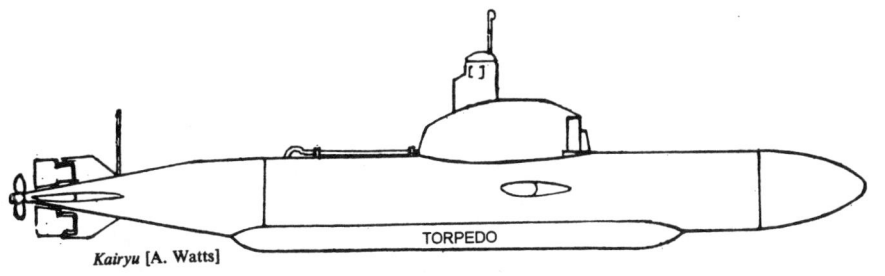

Kairyu [A. Watts]

Kairyu was a 2-man suicide mini-submarine with torpedos, one slung along each side. When torpedoes were short, the nose cone was filled with TNT.

would make wide-spread use of midget submarines, human torpedoes and exploding motorboats against the Americans.

Once offshore, the invasion fleet would be forced to defend not only against the suicide attacks from the air, but would also be confronted with suicide attacks from under the sea.

Attempting to sink our troop carrying transports, would be almost 300 Kairyu suicide submarines. These two-man subs carried a 1,320 pound bomb in their nose and were to be used in close-in ramming attacks. By the end of the war, the Japanese had 215 Kairyu available with 207 more under construction in eleven widely dispersed ship yards.

With a crew of five, the Japanese Koryu suicide submarine, carrying two 18-inch torpedoes, was also to be used against the American vessels. By August, the Japanese had 115 Koryu completed, with 496 under construction in nine different plants. (The *Kariyu* and the *Koryu* were different.)

Especially feared by our Navy were the Kaitens, which were difficult to detect. They were to be used against the American invasion fleet just off the beaches. These Kaitens were <u>human torpedoes</u> ranging between 48½ to 54 feet long (depending on the model of which there were two in production). Kaitens were propelled by hydrogen-peroxide engines. The Kaiten was efficient and deadly. The engine drove this torpedo at up to 40 knots though short ranged (about 24 miles) each carrying a warhead of over 3,500 tons of TNT. Each was capable of sinking the largest of Ameri-

35

can ships. The Japanese had built 419 Kaitens of which 78 were in the Kyushu area as early as August 1945.

Finally, the Japanese had almost 4,000 Navy and Army motor boats, which were also armed with high explosive war-heads, and which were to be used in nighttime attacks against American troop-carrying ships.

The principal goal of the special attack units of the air and of the sea was to shatter the invasion before the landing. By killing the combat troops aboard ships and sinking the attack transports and cargo vessels, the Japanese were convinced the Americans would back off or become so demoralized that they would then accept a less than uncondi-

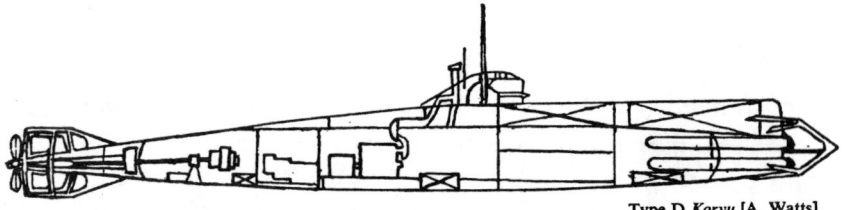

Type D *Koryu* [A. Watts]

Koryu was an operational 2-man "midget" submarine intended to be recoverd after a mission. A Koryu tried to get into Pearl Harbor on Dec. 7, 1941, was detected and sunk hours before the bombing. See picture page 38.

tional surrender and a more honorable and face-saving end for the Japanese.

In addition to destroying as many of the larger American ships as possible, "Ketsu-Go" also called for the annihilation of the smaller offshore landing craft carrying American soldier's to the invasion beaches.

The Japanese had devised a network of beach defenses. These consisted of electrically detonated mines farthest offshore, three lines of suicide divers, followed by magnetic mines and still other anti-personnel mines planted all over the beaches.

A fanatical part of the last line of maritime defense was the Japanese suicide frogmen, called "Fukuryu." These "crouching dragons" were divers armed with lunge mines,

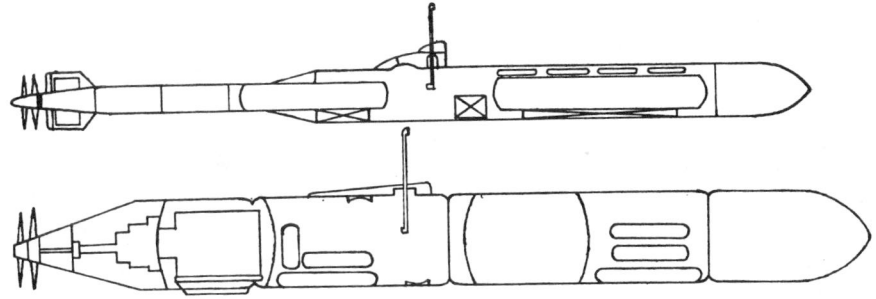

Kaiten I (upper), *Kaiten II* (lower) [A. Watts]

Kaiten, designed from a Type 93 torpedo, was first true suicide submarine; was armed with TNT. Due to shortage of engines, anticlimactic use was as fuel tanks on freighters.

Kaiten pilots like Lt. Maeda sought to forestall destruction of their country by sacrificing their lives in Samurai tradition.

—Orita

Kairyu (top) found at Yokosuka Navy Yard after the war. Koryu (lower) that attempted to enter Pearl harbor on December 7, 1941, was sunk outside harbor entrance before attack began; was first Japanese vessel sunk in WW-II by U.S.N. —U.S. Navy. This midget-sub was exhibited at Pearl Harbor for many years, has now been moved. —Orita.
(OPPOSITE PAGE) Artist's sketch (top) of attack method of Kaiten manned torpedoes. Kaitens mounted on mother-submarine's deck (center) were silently released from undersea. —Orita. Kaiten being released (lower) from destroyer *Kitakami* in February 1945. See page 40.
—Imperial War Museum

Kaitens or Koryu could be launched from destroyers.
See page 39. —Orita

each capable of sinking a landing craft up to 950 tons. The divers, numbering in the thousands, could stay submerged for up to ten hours, and were to thrust their explosive charges into the bottom of landing craft and, in effect, serve as human mines.

As horrible as the defense of Japan would be off the beaches, it would be on Japanese soil that the American armed forces would face the most rugged and fanatical defense that had ever been encountered in any of the theaters during the entire war.

Throughout the island-hopping Pacific campaign, American troops had always outnumbered the Japanese by two and some-times three to one. In Japan it would be different. By virtue of a combination of cunning, guesswork and brilliant military reasoning, a number of Japan's top military leaders were able to astutely deduce not only when, but where the United States would land their first invasion forces. The Japanese positioned their troops accordingly.

Facing the 14 American Divisions landing at Kyushu would be 14 Japanese Divisions, 7 independent mixed brigades, tank brigades and thousands of specially trained Naval Landing Forces. On Kyushu, the odds would be three to two in favor of the Japanese which would be ready with 790,000 defenders against 550,000 Americans. This time, the bulk of the Japanese defenders would not be the poorly trained and ill-equipped labor battalions that the Americans had faced in the earlier island campaigns. The Japanese defenders would be the hard core of the Japanese Home Army. These troops were fairly well fed and equipped, compared to the soldiers in the far-flung islands. These home troops all over Kyushu, were linked together not by hastily laid field telephone wires, but by instantaneous communications – radio. They were familiar with the terrain, had stockpiles of arms and ammunition, and had developed an effective system of transportation and re-supply almost invisible from the air. Some of these Japanese troops were the elite of the Japanese army. They were swollen with a fanatical fighting spirit that convinced them that they could defeat these American invaders that had come to defile their homeland.

Coming ashore, the American Eastern Amphibious Assault forces at Miyazaki (invasion beaches CHRYSLER, CORD, DESOTO, DUSSENBERG) would face the Japanese 154th Division, which straddled the city; the Japanese 212th Division on the coast immediately to the north, and the 156th Division on the coast immediately to the south. Also in place, and prepared to launch a counter-attack against the invading Eastern force, were the Japanese 25th and 77th Divisions.

Awaiting the Southeastern attack force at Ariake Bay (beaches WINTON, ZEPHYR, STUTZ) was the entire Japanese 86th Division, joined by at least one independent mixed infantry brigade.

On the western shores of Kyushu, the American Marines would face the most brutal of defenders. Along the invasion beaches would be the 146th, 206th and 303rd Japanese Divisions, along with the 6th Tank Brigade, the 125th Mixed Infantry Brigade and the 4th Artillery Command. Additionally, components of the 25th and 77th Divisions would also be poised to launch counterattacks.

If not needed to reinforce the primary landing beaches, the American Reserve Force would be landed at the base of Kagoshima by November 4th, where they would be immediately confronted by two mixed infantry brigades, parts of two infantry divisions and thousands of the naval landing forces that had undergone combat retraining to support ground troops in defense.

All along the invasion beaches, American troops would face coastal batteries, anti-landing obstacles, and an elaborate network of heavily fortified pillboxes, bunker strong points and underground fortresses.

As the American soldiers waded ashore, they would do so through intense artillery and mortar fire from preregistered batteries as they worked their way through tetrahedrons – pyramid-shaped underwater obstacles placed near beaches – and barbed wire entanglements so arranged to funnel the invaders into the muzzle of these Japanese guns.

On the beaches, and beyond, would be hundreds of Japanese machine gun positions, beach mines, booby traps, trip-wire mines, and sniper units. Suicide units concealed in spider holes would meet the troops as they approached. Just past the beaches and the sea walls, would be hundreds of barricades, trail blocks and concealed strong points.

In the heat of battle, Japanese infiltration units would be sent to reap havoc in the American lines by cutting field telephone lines, and by indiscriminately firing at Americans attempting to establish beachheads. Some Japanese would be in American uniforms to confuse the troops. English speaking Japanese were assigned to break in on American radio traffic to call off American artillery fire, to order retreats and to further confuse the invading forces.

Still other infiltrators with demolition charges strapped on their chests or backs would attempt to blow up American tanks, artillery pieces and ammunition stores as they were unloaded ashore.

were unloaded ashore.

Beyond the beaches, were large artillery pieces situated at key points to bring down a devastating curtain of fire on the avenues of approach along the beach. Some of these large guns were mounted on railroad cars whose tracks ran in to caves where they were protected by concrete and steel.

The battle for Japan, itself, would be won by what General Simon Bolivar Buckner had called on Okinawa "Prairie Dog Warfare." This type of fighting was almost unknown to the ground troops in Europe and the Mediterranean. It was peculiar only to the American soldiers and marines whose responsibility it had been to fight and destroy the Japanese on islands all over the south and central Pacific.

"Prairie Dog Warfare" had been the story of Tarawa, of Saipan, of Iwo Jima and Okinawa. "Prairie Dog Warfare" was a battle for yards, feet and sometimes even inches. It was a brutal, deadly and dangerous form of combat aimed at an underground, heavily fortified, non-retreating enemy.

The Americans might have tremendous resources in aircraft carriers, battleships, airplanes of all types, but it appears that the final victory would be the inch-by-inch "Prairie Dog Warfare" – rooting the enemy out of their caves one-at-a-time. This is what the invasion of Japan would be all about.

In the mountains behind the beaches were elaborate underground networks of caves, bunkers, command posts and hospitals. These were connected by miles of tunnels with dozens of separate entrances and exits. Some of these complexes could hold up to 1,000 enemy troops.

A number of these caves were equipped with large steel doors that slid open to allow artillery to fire, then the doors would snap shut. This "disappearing" artillery was not knew for the Americans had invented the principal at the turn of the century.*

* See the detailed accounts of the Coast Artillery Harbor Defense installations, with photographs, in *Silent Siege-III* in bibliography.

The paths leading to these underground fortresses were honeycombed with defensive positions. All but a few of the trails would be booby-trapped. Along these manned defensive positions, would be machine gun nests and non-flyable aircraft with good guns, as well as naval guns converted for anti-invasion firing.

In addition to the use of poison gas and bacteriological warfare (with which the Japanese had been experimenting), the most frightening of all was the prospect of meeting an entire civilian population that had been mobilized to meet the American troops on the beaches.

Had "Olympic" come about, the Japanese civilian population, inflamed by a national slogan:

ONE HUNDRED MILLION WILL DIE FOR THE EMPEROR AND NATION

...was prepared to engage and fight the American invaders to the death.

Twenty-eight million Japanese had become a part of the "National Volunteer Combat Force" and had undergone train-ing in the techniques of beach defense and guerrilla warfare. These civilians were armed with ancient rifles, lunge mines, satchel charges, Molotov cocktails and one-shot black powder mortars. Still others were armed with swords, long bows, axes and bamboo spears. These special civilian units were to be tactically employed in nighttime attacks, hit-and-run manoeuvres, delaying actions and massive suicide charges at the weaker American positions.

Even without the utilization of Japanese civilians in direct combat, the Japanese and American casualties during the campaign for Kyushu alone would have been staggering. At the early stage of the invasion, it was forecast that 1,000 Japanese and American soldiers would be dying every hour. The long and difficult task of conquering Kyushu would have made casualties on both sides enormous. One can only guess at how monumental the casualty figures would have been, on both sides, had the Americans repeated their invasion (Operation "Coronet") when they landed at the heavily fortified and defended Tokyo Plain the next March.

The invasion of Japan never became a reality because on August 6, 1945, the entire nature of war changed when the first atomic bomb used in war-time was exploded over Hiroshima. On August 9, 1945, a second bomb was dropped on Nagasaki. Within days, the war with Japan came to a stop.

Had these bombs not been dropped and had the invasion been launched as scheduled, it is hard not to speculate as to the cost. At the least, thousands of Japanese suicide sailors and airmen would have died fiery deaths in the defense of their homeland. Thousands of American sailors and airmen defending against these attacks would also have been killed with countless numbers wounded. As Americans were wounded and died in the surf and on the beaches, there would be little chance any if those hurt could be picked up by medics – themselves under fire and likewise, dying.

On the Japanese home islands, the combat casualties would have been at a minimum in the tens of thousands. Every foot of Japanese soil would have been paid for, twice over, by both Japanese and American lives.

One can only guess at how many civilians would have committed suicide, as recalled at Saipan, or in futile mass frontal attacks.

In retrospect, the one million American men who were to be the casualties of the invasion, were instead able to survive the war.

Intelligence studies and realistic military estimates made over forty years ago, and not latter day speculation, show quite clearly that the battle for Japan might well have resulted in the biggest bloodbath in the history of modern warfare.

> At best, the invasion of Japan would have resulted in a long and bloody siege. At worst, it could have been a battle of extermination between two different civilizations.

45

Far worse would be what might have happened to Japan as a nation and as a culture. When the invasion came, it would have come after several additional months of the continued fire bombings on all of the remaining Japanese cities and population centers.

The cost in human life from the fire bombings in Japan in March of 1945, come to mind where far more were killed by these conventional bombings and in the fires that followed than were killed by American atomic bombs at Hiroshima and at Nagasaki.

The deaths at Hiroshima and at Nagasaki that resulted from the two atomic blasts would be small in comparison to the total number of Japanese lives that would have been lost during a continuing aerial devastation.

If the invasion had come in the fall of 1945, with the American forces locked in combat in the south of Japan, who or what could have prevented the Red Army from marching into the northern half of the Japanese home islands? If "Downfall" had been an operational necessity, the existence of a separate North and South Japan might have become a post-war reality.

In that scenario, Japan today could be divided somewhere across its middle much like Korea continues to be and as Germany had been during the occupation of the Soviets. The world was spared the cost of "Downfall," however, because on September 2, 1945, Japan formally surrendered to the United Nations and World War II became history.

Almost immediately, American soldiers, sailors, airmen and marines busy in their branches of service for "the duration and six months" were starting to be sent home. The aircraft carriers, cruisers, transport ships and LST's scheduled to carry American invasion troops in the conquest of Japan, now ferried American troops homeward in a gigantic troop-lift called "Magic Carpet."

The soldiers and marines who had been committed to invade Japan, were now thinking of life outside of a uniform and having to listen to barked orders from superiors. All over America, celebrations were held and families everywhere gathered in thanksgiving to honor their soldiers who had been miraculously spared from further combat.

In the fall of 1945, with the war now over, few Americans would ever learn of the elaborate *TOP SECRET* plans that had been prepared in fine detail for the invasion of Japan. Those few military leaders who had known the details of "Operation "Downfall" were now busy with plans for the official occupation of Japan.

After the war closed, due directly to the employment of the two atomic bombs, few people were concerned about the invasion plans that had been rendered obsolete by the arrival of the Atomic Age. After the surrender, all of the classified documents, maps, and details for "Operation Downfall" were packed away in boxes where they would remain classified and stored first at the War Department, then eventually into the collection of the National Archives where they still remain.

Even now, a half-century later, these plans that called for the invasion of Japan paint a vivid description of what might have been one of the most horrible campaigns in the history of modern man. The fact that "Operation Downfall," the story of the invasion of Japan, is not reflected in our history books is something for which all Americans can be thankful. ☐

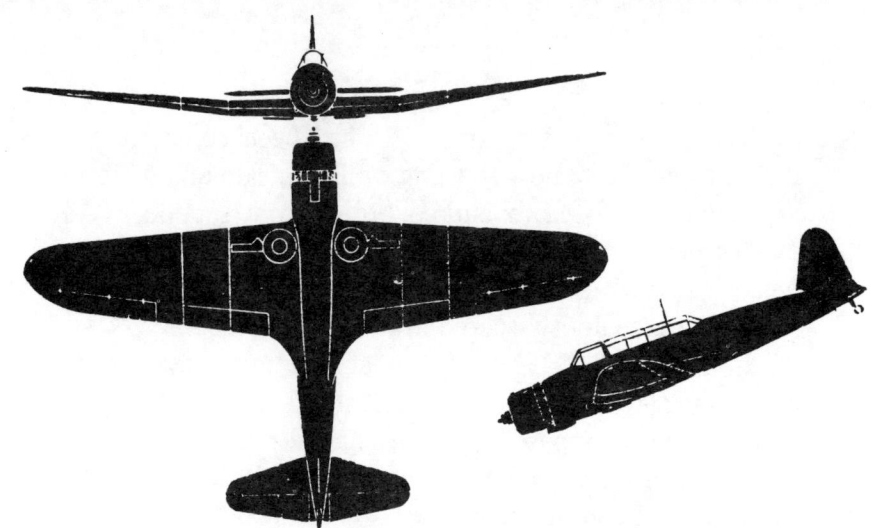

The Navy 97 Mk. III Torpedo-Bomber "Kate."

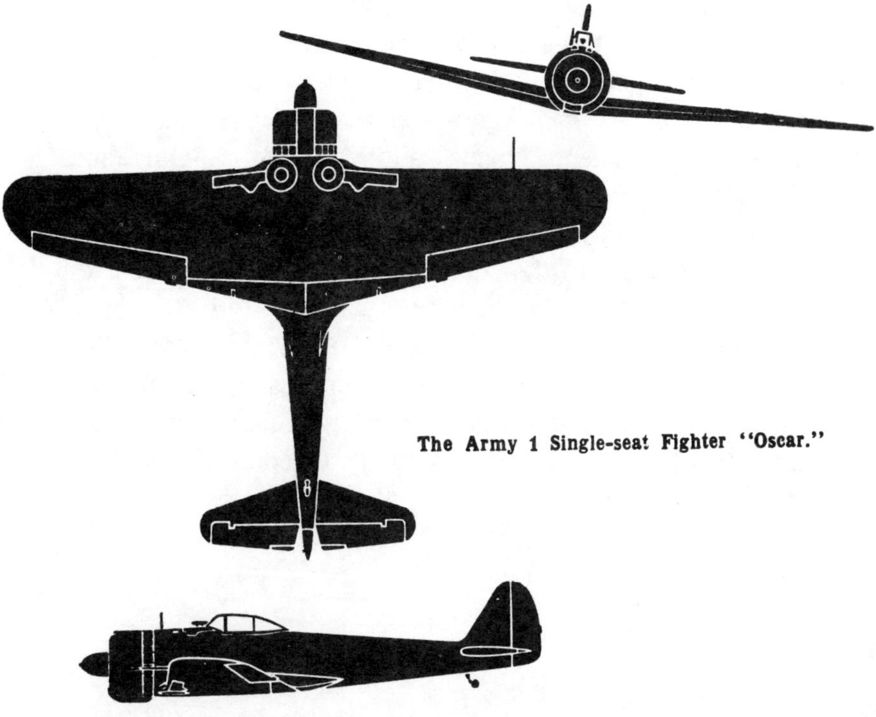

The Army 1 Single-seat Fighter "Oscar."

All Japanese fighter or torpedo planes were good for Kamikaze missions. Many pilots, successful with regular bombing or dog-fight sorties, returned to base to fly another day. Some flyable but otherwise damaged planes were designated for 1-way Kamikaze missions.

—U.S. Navy.

Kamikaze Suicide Planes
Attack American Ships

American experiences with the Kamikaze's during the battle off Samar (October 25, 1944) may provide a clue as to what could be expected by flights of Japanese suicide planes during the American all-out invasion of the Japanese home islands. For our example, here are excerpts based on Admiral Samuel Eliot Morison's account.*

---

* From Vol. XIV. *See* bibliography

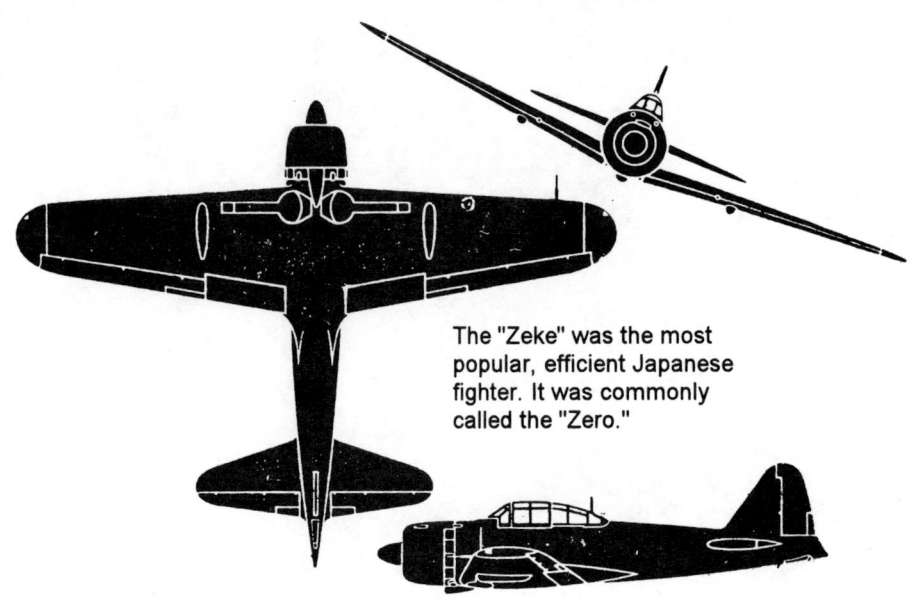

The "Zeke" was the most popular, efficient Japanese fighter. It was commonly called the "Zero."

The Navy O Single-engined Fighter ''Zeke.''

The carrier *Santee* had just finished launching five TBM's and eight FM-25's when a Japanese plane dove onto her out of a cloud, and so near that no guns could be brought to bear. It came in strafing, crashed the flight deck on the port side forward and continued on through the hangar deck. The explosion blew a hole 15 by 30 feet, and started fires in the immediate vicinity of eight 1,000-pound bombs. The failure of these bombs to detonate is probably the most fortunate event in *Santee's* long and active career. The fire was brought under control by 0751 but the carrier sustained 43 casualties, 16 of them fatal.

Half a minute after this suicide crash, another Kamikaze circled *Suwannee* astern, and, when hit by her antiaircraft fire, spiraled down and rolled over into a dive, heading for *Sangamon.* One 5-inch shell fired by *Suwannee* hit the plane when it was about 500 feet from her sister flattop, causing the airplane to swerve and splash into the sea at a safe distance. At the same time, *Petrof Bay* was closely missed by a third Kamikaze which was knocked down by shells from antiaircraft fire.

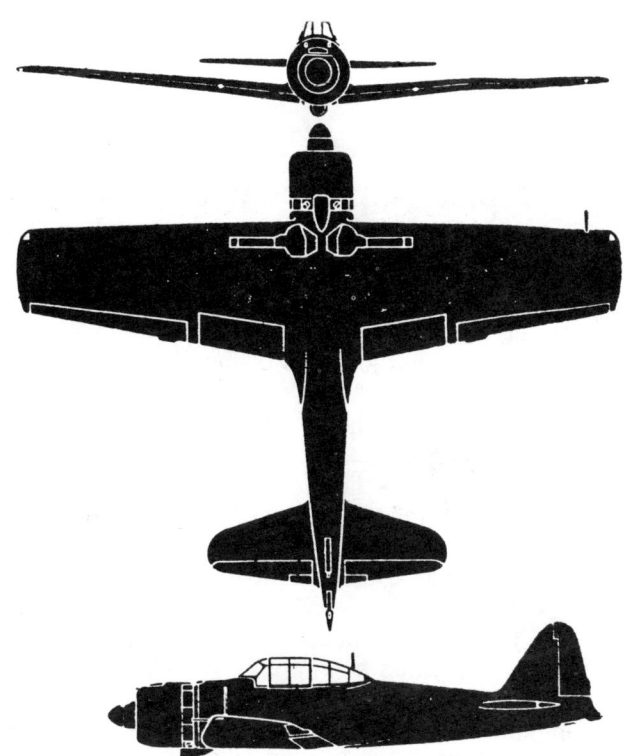

The Navy O Mk. II Single-engined Fighter "Hamp."

Five minutes after the fire had been extinguished on *Santee,* she was hit on the starboard side a torpedo that had been launched by Japanese submarine *I-56.* The explosion caused some damage, but no casualties. *I-56* had picked the wrong ship, for this large converted tanker of this class safely absorbed hits that would have been lethal to the lighter Kaiser class. *Santee,* with a slight list from flooding, was making 16½ knots before eight bells struck.

Suwannee, after shooting down two Zekes, spotted a third off her stern circling in the clouds at 8,000 feet altitude. Her antiaircraft gunners were on it in a jiffy. The plane rolled over, smoking, toward the carrier's starboard side and then plummeted, hitting *Suwannee* about 40 feet forward of the after elevator. This crash made a 10-foot hole in the flight deck. Its bomb exploded between the flight and hangar decks, tearing a 25-foot hole in the latter, which

Typical Approaches for Kamikaze Pilots

The schemes for attacking the American ships was two-fold:
1.) From high altitude, usually diving out of the sun. 2.) From low altitude barely skimming the surface of the sea.

In the earliest days of the Kamikazes, the high level sheme was common but lookouts of the ships, having been trained to look "high and wide" spotted the divng airplanes even when the planes were backlighted by the sun. And radar also picked them up easily.

The low-level tactic proved to be much more effective. The pilot had two choices.
1.) He could drive his bomb-laden airplane directly into the side of the ship, usually at the bridge level.
2.) He might do a modified high-level attack. If he chose the latter, his wave-top skipping under radar flight would continue to about 1,500 yards away from the target vessel when he would pull the stick back. Then, with full throttle, do a near-vertical climb to an altitude of about 1,000 to 1,500 feet where he would level off. From this vantage point, the pilot sized up his target, dumped his nose while pointing his plane at his target, held a steady course in the power dive to crash the ship.

Low-level approach

On some buddy-system attacks, the lookouts and gunners on the target ship would be distracted when two Kamikazies, one coming in from high-level and the other on a low-level approach at the same time. By war's end, over 2,500 pilots were killed by purposely crashing their planes into American targets.

—Computer-assisted sketch by Bert Webber

The *USS Suwannee* after being hit by Kamikaze in Battle off Samar – 85 sailors were killed, 58 missing, 102 wounded. (Photo made from *USS Santee*.) (Lower) Damage to forward elevator after the fire was out. —U.S. Navy.

The *USS Fanshaw Bay* (in distance) after Kamikaze attack as view from flight deck of *USS Kitkun Bay*. Airplanes on deck are F4F Wildcat fighters.   —U.S. Navy.

damaged the main deck and caused a number of casualties.

The fire on the hangar deck was promptly quenched but the after plane elevator remained inoperative. Within two hours, the flight deck damage had been temporarily repaired so landings could again be made. At 1009, air operations were resumed.

Five Japanese aircraft from Luzon, jumped the American carriers at 1050 hours just as the carriers, respited from enemy gunfire, were trying to recover their own aircraft. These Kamikazes never did show on the radar as they approached from very low altitude. Then they climbed rapidly inside SK radar range, and started dives from 5,000 to 6,000 feet. So sharp and sudden was their onslaught, that C.A.P. was unable to intercept.

Kitkun Bay, Admiral Ofstie's flagship, caught the first attack. A Zeke, crossing her bow from port to starboard, climbed rapidly, rolled and dove directly at the bridge, strafing as he came. The plane missed the bridge, passed over the island, crashed the port catwalk and bounced into

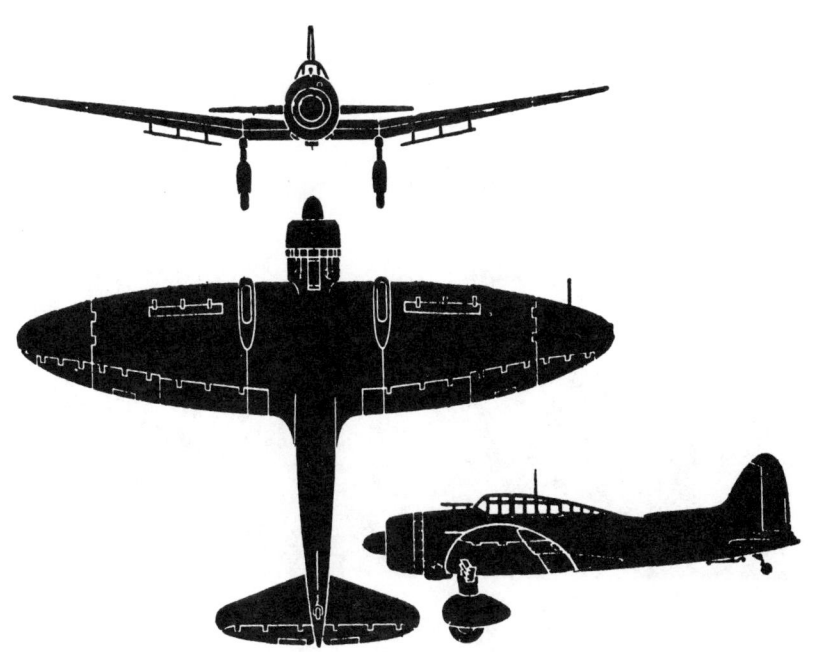
The Navy 99 Mk. II Dive-Bomber "Val."

the sea. But the bomb that it carried exploded, causing much damage.

Two of the Kamikazes went for *Fanshaw Bay,* but both were shot down. The other two dove toward *White Plains.* At an altitude of 500 feet, they pulled out of their dive, both under fire by 40-mm guns. The one that was already smoking, turned and dove onto *St. Lo.*

Captain McKenna had secured from General Quarters and set Condition II to give the men a chance to rest and down some hot coffee. Lookouts on the *St.* Lo sighted these planes at 1051 and immediately opened fire. But the Zeke which had her number crashed through the flight deck and burst into flames below. Quickly, there followed seven explosions of torpedoes and bombs on the hangar deck. Great sections of the flight deck and elevator and entire airplanes were hurled hundreds of feet into the air. The ship blazed from stem to stern, and at 1125, the *St. Lo* foundered under a cloud of dense smoke."

USS St. Lo blows up after attack. This U.S. carrier was sunk by Kamikaze. Rescue ships picked up 754 survivors, many badly wounded.   —U.S. Navy.

The second member of this Kamikaze pair partly circled the formation, turned, and started a run on *White Plains* which maneuvered to evade with hard left rudder. The plane came in weaving under intense fire of all after guns. A torrent of blazing tracers could be seen entering its fuselage and wing roots. When only a few yards astern, the plane rolled over and dove, missing the port catwalk by inches and exploded between that level and the water. The flight deck was showered with debris and a blast of sticky fragments of the pilot. Eleven men on the ship were injured.

As *Kitkun Bay* was steaming on course 200° at 1110 hours, she sighted 15 Judys approaching the formation from astern, distant about five miles. She launched two Wildcats (F4F's) by catapult for combat air patrol, but not in time. This ship, and the three remaining carriers, *Fanshaw Bay*,

Nagatsuka, a Japanese fighter
pilot, (top) in Sept. 1944 and
(right) in Jan. 1945. Plane
(lower) is Kawasaki Ki-61 Hien
fighter used on Kamikaze
missions. —Nagatsuka

White Plains and *Kitkun Bay* were without a screen, owing to rescue work.

One of three Kamikazes got through the C.A.P. and dove at *Kitkun Bay* from astern. Its wings were shot off as it neared the ship, and just in time, for the bomb the plane dropped struck the water 25 yards on the star-board bow then parts of the plane hit the forecastle. *Kitkun Bay* received a crash dive on her flight deck which damaged it badly, but the fires that started were put out in less than five minutes. A second plane crashed her after stack and two others dove but missed. Admiral Sprague's flagship, the lucky *Fannie Bee*, alone sustained no damage in this assault.

The U. S. Navy realized it was now confronted with a new challenge in air defense – Kamikaze suicide pilots. Until after these attacks, nobody realized here was the beginning of new and desperate tactics on the part of the Japanese. The prospects were distinctly unpleasant. □

Pilot Ryuji Nagatsuka, in his book, *I Was A Kamikaze* (see bibliography) said on orders from the High Command, "all pilots were to be trained to become human torpedoes, to evade enemy fire, to crash exactly on target, the goal 'one plane for one ship.'" He declared that he and his fellow pilots were "neither coerced nor brainwashed into volunteering for Kamikaze missions, that they all volunteered willingly, eagerly, to save family and fatherland."

Air-To-Air Kamikaze

The Lieutenant addressed the Cadet Corps saying, "It is urgent that we use all the aircraft at our disposal so as to wipe out the greatest possible number if these American bombers. Even though all of you are not fully trained, what counts is neither the skill of the pilot nor the quality of the airplane. The important thing is the spirit and the moral of you men."

The officer was an expert with the *Kai-45*. It was a heavy airplane and admittedly a hard plane to fly. But with his *Kai*, he had shot down more than 10 B-29's. For the next sortie, some of the cadets were to go aloft with the smaller *Kai-27's*. As the Superfortresses had been flying over Kyushu at much lower altitudes, the *Ki-27* could attack at 16,000 feet altitude. The others cadets will take the *Kai-45's* higher then descend to join the smaller fighters. The plan was to get in as close as possible to the bombers to be effective.

When the alert sounded that B-29's were in the distance, Flight Sergeant Nonaka ran to his *Kai-45* without putting on his flying suit and took off with his engine not even warmed up. His usual wing-man was closely behind. It took about half-an-hour to stalk the B-29, which Nonaka attacked from the rear-below angle. He purposely, with full throttle, crashed his *Kai* against the huge bomber at an altitude of about 25,000 feet. The two airplanes, stuck together and now engulfed in a single roaring flame, dropped out of the sky like a rock. Back at the air field, his buddy reported, "This method of attack, even though you risk almost certain death, it not as easy as it looks. But Nonaka was successful. He sacrificed himself for a Superfortress and its crew."

—Adapted from Nagatsuka, see bibliography

The Japanese Atomic Bomb
and Its Intended Use

The information put together by James Martin Davis about the plans for the American invasion of Japan, has caused many readers to have sleepless nights. Since his work originated in 1986, additional data has now been discovered.

Yes, The Japanese Had an Atomic Bomb !

There is a movement throughout the world, particularly in the United States, with considerable following in Japan, that the use of the atomic bombs on Hiroshima and on Nagasaki was not needed to end the war and that such use, from a humanitarian standpoint, was ill-advised.

Wrong because the huge explosions were so devastating, killed so many persons, and destroyed so much property.

But have those who pursue the "anti-nuke" persuasion studied closely about the reasons for the use of these horrendous bombs?

What might have happened to the United States and to Japan if these atomic bombs had not been used?

It is not our plan here to provide pages and pages of arguments about the philosophy for using or not using such explosives as there are countless pages written about this already to the point of *ad nauseum*.

But what about "new" information?

On the day of the Nagasaki bombing:

The Japanese High Command secretly tested its own atomic bomb.

At dawn on that day, a small remote-controlled motor boat, bearing the Japanese answer to Hiroshima, was sent against a small island in the Sea of Japan. This experiment was unannounced.

The blast leveled the target and vaporized dozens of fishing boats and the occupants who happened to be there. The Japanese had experimented on its own people.

Word of the Nagasaki destruction captured the newspaper headlines of the day. Nothing was printed regarding the successful Japanese test as the High Command didn't tell anyone about it.

The Japanese "A-bomb" was of a low-yield intensity compared with the American high-yield bombs. While the American bombs were very large and heavy, and would devastate a wide area, reliable report indicates the Japanese version could fit into a cigar box.

The Japanese apparently had no intention of developing a bomb that would level entire cities, as happened at Hiroshima then Nagasaki. The reasons for this are arguable, and plausibly a major reason was that the Japanese had only a scant supply of uranium and sought to construct several small bombs with what they had.

From the book *Silent Siege-III*, we see that the Japanese and Germans were "buddies" on exchanges of some technology and supplies – the shipments going between the counties by submarines. From the same source we find that a German U-boat, the *U*-235 surrendered in the Atlantic ocean at the end of the European war. It was escorted into the Portsmouth Naval Base at Kittery, Maine, by a U. S. Navy Destroyer Escort. The *U*-235 had a large stock of uranium on board as well as a great shipment of Mercury. Also on board were two high-ranking Japanese scientists returning home from "business" in Germany. Just before the *U*-235 surrendered, these two Japanese killed themselves to avoid

1.) To save face for failing their Emperor
2.) To avoid capture, with a load of uranium, by the Americans

It appears that in the pre-war period of the theoretical study of nuclear physics, the Japanese and other scientists, the total of these men being small, all were fairly well known to each other. The Japanese, being keen on details, had a duplicate of the cyclotron whose sister was at the University of California.

How did the Japanese get it?

They bought it.

Accordingly, data about the smashing of the atom was not unknown to the Japanese. In fact, any member of the public who was interested, attended the public demonstrations about "atom smashing," as it was called, at the Worlds Fair at Treasure Island at San Francisco in 1939. When the fair was held over for another season – 1940 – again, anyone interested in the budding science of nuclear physics could attend the shows for the admission price to the fair. (The editor of this book attended these talks several times.)

When war between Japan and the United States started – December 7th, 1941 "A date that will live in infamy"* –

---

* Pearl Harbor Day, December 7, has been declared "National Pearl Harbor Remembrance Day." Without public notice and without news media representatives present, President Bill Clinton signed *Public Law 108-308 August 23, 1994*. Lillian Baker, a World War II war-widow and much-published historian, was the spearhead for this new law back in 1972. In a special letter to her from the Architect of the Capitol, a special flag, that was flown on the day of signing, was sent to her as a gift commemorating the event.

NATIONAL PEARL HARBOR REMEMBRANCE DAY
PROCLAMATION

Joint Resolution designating December 7 of each year as "National Pearl

all discussions on all subjects between the two nations stopped. What the Japanese did from that date until after the war was concluded, about their nuclear interests, was unknown to the so-called "out-side world." American General Leslie R. Groves, Corps of Engineers, who was in charge of the American "Manhattan Project," the building of the American atomic bomb, played down, when interviewed after the war, about what the Japanese knew about nuclear physics. He indicated he didn't think the Japanese had scientists of sufficient knowledge to pursue the matter. He also knew that Japan was not a Uranium producing country to the extent needed for any bomb building.

Harbor Remembrance Day."

Whereas, on December 7, 1941, the Imperial Japanese Navy and Air Force attacked units of the armed forces of the United States stationed at Pearl Harbor, Hawaii;

Whereas more than 2,000 citizens of the United States were killed and more than 1,000 citizens of the United States were wounded in the attack on Pearl Harbor;

Whereas the attack on Pearl Harbor marked the entry of the United States into World War II;

Whereas the veterans of World War II and all other people of the United States commemorate December 7 in remembrance or the attack on Pearl Harbor; and

Whereas commemoration of the attack on Pearl Harbor will instill in all people of the United States a greater understanding and appreciation of the selfless sacrifice of the Individuals who served in the armed forces of the United States during World War II: Now, therefore, be it

Resolved by the Senate and House of Representatives of the United States of America in Congress assembled, That December 7 of each Year is designated as "National Pearl Harbor Remembrance Day" and the President is authorized and requested—

(1) to issue annually a proclamation calling on the people of the United States to observe the day with appropriate ceremonies and activities; and

(2) to urge all Federal agencies, and interested organizations, groups and individuals, to fly the flag of the United States at half-staff each December 7 in honor of the Individuals who individuals who died as a result of their service a Pearl Harbor.

Approved August 23, 1994.

108 STAT. 1669
—From Jackson County Law Library – Medford, Oregon Nov. 11, 1994

Blessed with the vision of "20-20-Hindsight," the American scientific community realized after the war that Japan had indeed been lurking in the shadows with atomic bomb developments all during the Pacific War. Where had the work been going on? In Korea.

Two questions come to mind:

1.) What targets would the Japanese consider for its A-bombs?
2.) By what method would such bombs be delivered?

The Japanese were excellent in the design and construction of submarines. Mitsubishi Heavy Industries was a prime contractor. When the *I-400* series of submarines was planned, these vessels would be over-grown models of the *I-15* class. The *I-15* class vessels were noted for being very long range. We recall that *I-25*, drove from Yokosuka to the West Cost of the United States and back again and still had fuel in its tanks. But of immense surprise to the Americans, *I-25* was an "aircraft-carrying" submarine. It's Yokosuka E-14Y1 aircraft (Allied code name GLEN), was successfully launched from its deck, flew over Southern Oregon, dropped bombs in the Siskiyou National Forest and started a forest fire. This fete was on September 9, 1942.

Ah so!

High-speed fighter/bomber designed for *I-400* class submarines.
—U.S. Navy.

The *I-400* class subs, which were designed to reach New York non-stop from Japan, would carry *three* airplanes – the Japanese named the planes SEIRAN.

The alleged plan was to drop atomic bombs on the locks of the Panama Canal. This would instantly kill everyone around and close the canal for years.

As the war's end grew closer, Japan's ability to deliver the bomb was weakening by the week. Japan was being so heavily bombed with high explosives and so many of its ships were being sunk at sea, that when the time came, the Japanese had trouble finding enough diesel fuel to handle daily operations, let along supply a fleet to cross the Pacific Ocean to within striking distance of the canal. (One of the few *I-400's* built, had to go to China for fuel for a mission to Ulithi.) Further, the new bomb wasn't quite ready.

*   *   *

When the American troops stormed toward the Kyushu beaches on November 1, 1945, the plan was for the Japanese to let the invasion proceed to a certain point just off-shore, then with Kamikazes, shower the invaders with low-level atomic bombs. It was estimated each bomb would kill about 10,000 American infantrymen, along with the Kamikaze pilot, in a split second.

So, here comes the invading Americans —Pooph!— and the attackers are pulverized. Pooph again, and another

10,000 American soldiers are dust! All along the beaches:

Pooph!
Pooph!
Pooph!

> The awful truth of what war is all about is that it is killing people. Do I have a right to that opinion? Yes. I commanded a rifle company in combat in Africa and Italy, was on the Anzio Beachhead, the breakout and the Italian campaign through its entirety. I have the combat infantry badge and two Purple Hearts. I believe that I know what war and battles are all about.
> —Christian P. Hald, M.D. (Colonel, Infantry - Retired) *See:* bibliography

If Operation "Olympic" failed due to the Japanese atomic bombs, would the United States have dared to launch Operation "Cononet"?

While the American public had been nearly unanimous about supporting the war effort for four trying years, would the public have risen and demanded an immediate end to the war if "Operation Olympic" had failed? What kind of a surrender would have been written in the face of a million or more American casualties? Would Japan and the United States come to terms in order to preserve each other?

Would Edward Kintoku Ige's proclamation be realized:

Before this war is over you watch – California will belong to Japan !*

Because the explosion of the American A-bombs on Japanese cities had brought Japan to surrender on its knees, the questions would never be asked.

But the reality of Hiroshima and Nagasaki is clear –

* Ige was a Japanese-American who declared he would not fight in the U.S. Army under any conditions but would readily fight in the Japanese Army against the U.S. "and kill some of these white b------. I am not scared of any white man.... Some day I would like to have a bunch of white servants working for me. Before this war is over you watch, California will belong to Japan!" If Ige was living on August 10, 1988, the day Public Law 100-383 was signed by President Reagan, he was sent a check for $20,000 and an "apology for his human suffering" from the people of the United States.

66

very clear.

The Japanese started the war with the unannounced attacks on Pearl Harbor and on the Philippines.

The United States ended the war with the unannounced attacks on Hiroshima and on Nagasaki.

In war, one does what one has to do.

> An infantryman can say, 'I have been there.' The infantrymen I know also say, 'Once is enough.' For the final assault on Japan, I was to command Company I, 361st Infantry, a first wave rifle company. What would my chances of survival have been? No one knows. But I believe that they would not have been good. Must we continue to apologize to ourselves and to the Japanese for saving millions of lives by our use of the A-bombs? I think not.   —Christian P. Hald, M.D. (Colonel, Infantry - Retired)
>
> *See:* bibliography

As a result of the timely uses of the American atomic bombs, thousands upon thousands – millions of American as well as Japanese lives – were saved because the Americans did not have to invade the Japanese home islands.

Preserve the Peace
So we don't have to
Pickup the pieces
—Bert Webber

Appendix A

The Japanese Bombing Balloons

An example of one of the stranger occurrences about the war, where military historian personnel abandoned their work and went home when the war was over, deals with the fact that the Japanese had engaged in a serious effort to burn down the timber industry of the Pacific Northwest. This included Oregon, Idaho Washington, Montana, as well as British Columbia. The Japanese method for this effort was truly enterprising and unique. They were vigorously sending at least 30,000 incendiary bombs, dangling beneath huge hydrogen-filled paper balloons, launched in the home islands, by way of the jet stream, to automatically drop in and fire American forests. These balloons were 70-feet high and floated above the limits of nearly all U.S. fighter planes.

The methods and details about these mysterious attacks, were only partially known to the American and Canadian authorities by the end of the war. What little was known was quickly lost in the files.

> → The same lack of interest kept the plans for the invasion of the Japanese home islands by American GI's in files that soon became just as dusty.

Was everything about the Japanese bombing attacks against the mainland of the United States learned by war's end, or did the military intelligence people just want to go home as the war was over so forget it? They just stopped looking.

There was nothing substantial published about these attacks – which including the killing of children in Oregon as a direct result of Japanese action – for another thirty years.

It has been claimed that if these attacks had happened along the Atlantic coast, there would have been, in the last fifty years, at least one-hundred books about them. But as this was a West coast event, and in the "lonely far North-west corner that nobody knows or cares about anyway," only one writer has dug it all out.

When Bert Webber was commissioned to write about the Japanese attacks along the Northwest coast by the Oregon State System of Higher Education through Oregon State University Press, it was a mandate of the Board of Governors that the work be so thorough that no other writer would be left any room to compete. And so it is a fact that Bert Webber's work has never been seriously challenged since the day in 1975 when it was first published.

When the research of this topic started in 1972, there was very little data found in the official records, as collecting and cataloging the information had promptly stopped once the war was over. And fewer still were the people who had participated in the events both in the U. S. and in Japan who remembered any of the details. Those who could be found contributed what they knew to piece the puzzle together. Webber's research turned up dozens of "post-war incidents" as recently as summer of 1992.

Has the work been updated? When OSU-Press released its interests back to the author, Webber created updates under different publishers in 1984, 1988 and in December 1992.

*   *   *

It serves to summarize the Japanese attacks against the mainland of the United States and Canada here.

These attacks started within a few days of the strike on Pearl Harbor when Japanese submarines were sinking ships within sight of the beaches of the West coast states. In 1942, there was another incident in February where an oil field in Southern California was shelled by the heavy gun on Imperial Japanese submarine *I-17* (Commander Nishino). Then in June, the *I-25* (Commander Tagami) shot up Fort Stevens at the mouth of the Columbia River. Just the night before, *I-26* (Commander Yokoda) shot at the lighthouse on Estevan Point on the West coast of Vancouver Island. Then *I-25* came back and twice in September launched its airplane.

–Yes! The Japanese had aircraft carrying submarines!

On the first of two bombing runs, the Japanese pilot (Fujita) bombed the Siskiyou National Forest. His bombs started a forest fire.

The year 1943 was quiet although the 1942 activities along the West coast of the U. S. caused many thousands of American troops to be tied up there, on the alert as lookouts for an invasion by the Japanese that, fortunately, never materialized.

Late in the year 1944 and into spring of 1945, incendiary bombs started falling out of the sky by the hundreds. *One bomb killed kids in Oregon.* In all, the Japanese were successful in landing bombs, bomb fragments and parts of broken flying apparatus, all from the stratosphereic flying balloons, in 28 states and Alaska, Canada, and in Mexico.

"Silence – the best defense!" By arrangement, American newspaper and radio news editors kept their mouths shut so as not to panic the American people and so the Japanese, through diplomatic channels, would not learn that they were being successful. See the book *Silent Siege-III*.

The American government was so nervous about the plausibility of an invasion of the West coast, that two severe measures were taken:

1.) Parts or all of the West coast states and Arizona were declared "Military areas" from which all persons who were citizens of nations with which the U.S. was at war, were invited to remove themselves. This specifically included Germans, Italians and Japanese.

In the case of the Japanese, there was a unique matter to be faced. All Japanese children were considered by Japan to be citizens of Japan regardless of where in the world they might have been born. But under American law, having been born in the U.S.A., they were American citizens. Thus, there were many thousands of persons of Japanese descent along the West coast of the U. S., who had "dual-citizenship."

When Japanese boys reached age 17, they were obligated to serve in the Japanese Army. When war came to the United States by Japan's attack on Pearl Harbor, December 7, 1941, the Japanese-American boys were faced with a terrible question: Would they serve the Emperor, or would these boys serve the land of their birth, the United States? As history shows, most of the boys chose the United States. But many others favored Japan and a large number set out, after the war started, to be disruptive to the American war effort. These young men were segregated from the general ethnic population and confined in the Tule Lake Segregation Center at Newell, California. This was in the far northeastern corner of California near the Oregon border.

While there, many hundreds said they wished to denounce their American citizenship stating they wanted to join the Japanese army to fight against America. They were allowed to give up their American citizenship by a special Act of Congress. But they were held at the Center until the war was over, then, enmasse, they were deported to Japan.

To ease the threat of Japanese in America from helping the Emperor's forces in event of invasion anywhere along the West coast, and to make certain that the dual-citizen Japanese-Americans did not join their parents who were mostly Japanese Nationals (enemy aliens), in aiding the enemy, all persons of Japanese ancestry were relocated to temporary housing centers inland. It is true therefore, that the relocation of Germans, Italians and Japanese – especially the Japanese – from the restricted areas was a military necessity and had nothing to do with race.

Was there a real or just an imagined threat that the Japanese locals would side with an invading enemy?

The U. S. Army Signal Corps had broken the Japanese diplomatic code just before the war started. Accordingly, the United States was able to "read the mail" of the Japanese. Among the messages, were lists of names and addresses of Japanese along the West coast of the U. S. that the Japanese government would be counting on for "aid."

Immediately after the war started, the F.B.I and Federal Marshalls, swooped down and arrested hundreds of Japanese who had been specifically identified in the "MAGIC" messages from the broken code. These men were taken to Department of Justice Internment Camps. Hearings were held. If a man was determined to be innocent, he was paroled. If not, he sat out the war then all who had been interned were deported.

2.) If there was an invasion on the American West coast and the meager forces there were over-run by the enemy Japanese, the American national stand would be in the Rocky Mountains. In other words, if the war came to the shores of the U.S.A., along its West coast, and the situation became untenable, the government was ready to write off San Diego, Los Angeles, Santa Barbara, San Francisco, Sacramento, Portland, Seattle, and all points in between.

The factors mentioned here have been largely dismissed as "science fiction" or, in the case of the Japanese-Americans, so blown out of shape by "politically correct historians," who are making a tireless effort at re-writing

American history, that most of what has been popularly published is not just badly warped but is grossly lacking in truth.

Books of significance about the Japanese-American experience, based on untarnished documents from the National Archives and other sources, are these works by Lillian Baker. These titles are presently available.

American and Japanese Relocation in World War II, Fact, Fiction & Fallacy (Webb Research Group Publishers, 1989)

The japanning of America; Redress & Reparations Demands by Japanese-Americans (Webb Research Group Publishers, 1991);

Dishonoring America; The Falsifying of World War II History (Webb Research Group Publishers, 1994).

Appendix B

Naval Personnel on Active Duty at End of August 1945 and Presumed to be Available for "Operation Downfall"

Naval Officers (Male)	316,675
Naval Officers (Female)	8,399
Total Officers	325,074
Nurses	10,968
Personnel in Officer Training Programs (Male)	69,913
Personnel in Officer Training Programs(Female)	12
Enlisted Personnel (Men)	2,935,695
Enlisted Personnel (Female)	73,685
Total Navy Personnel	3,408,347
Marine Corps	
Officers (Men)	36,851
Officers (Female)	813
Total Marine Corps including those in schools	485,833
Coast Guard	
Officers (Men)	11,766
Officers (Female)	855
Total Coast Guard including those in schools	170,275
Grand Total of Personnel under Navy Control	4,064,455

—Annual Report of the Secretary of the Navy, 10 January 1946.

Appendix C

Airplanes and Routes For Air Transport of Troops to Japan

As we have seen:

...divisions redeployed from Europe, and undergoing training in the United States, would be shipped to Japan in what was hoped to be the final push.

If the American invasion of Japan got into trouble, the back-up reserves in the United States would have to be deployed rapidly. The active word here is "rapidly." But this was World War II days and troop movements were about 99 percent by ships moving slowly in convoys. While a convoy speed of probably 12 to 15 knots might be maintained with fairly new "Victory" ships, if there were any "Liberty" ships hauling heavy goods, as part of the convoy, the speed was reduced in half. Neither of these speeds seemed conducive toward moving troops from the U.S. to Japan in a hurry.

Therefore the question: What about *flying* the troops and their equipment? Some limited troop air transport had been undertaken in the buildup in England prior to the Normandy Invasion. But only about 1 percent of the American personnel going to England flew there. These were primarily officers. What airplanes did the U. S. have that could ferry troops in quantity?

The most-ready and available airplane for this assignment was the Douglas C-54 "Skymaster." The C-54 was a 4-engine over-sized C-47 (DC-3). It could cruise at 222 miles per hour and had a maximum range of about 3,500

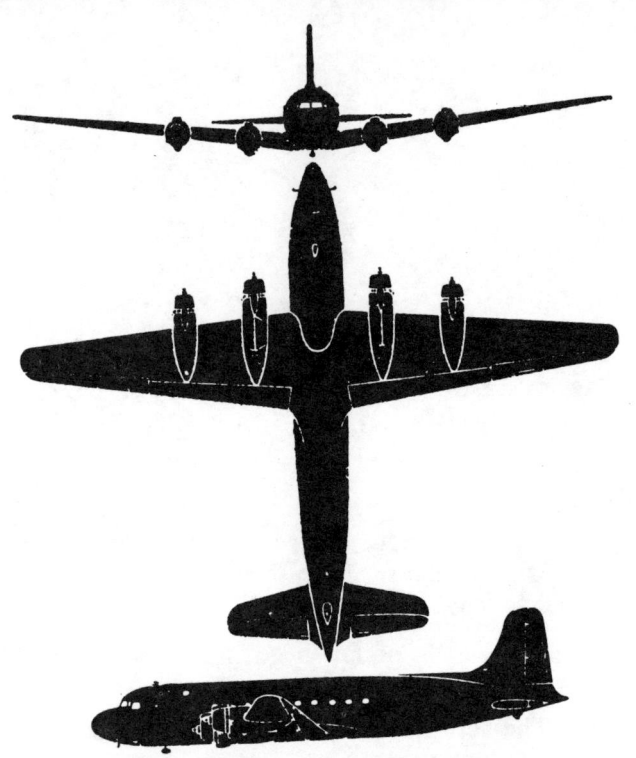

The Douglas ''Skymaster'' Military Transport.

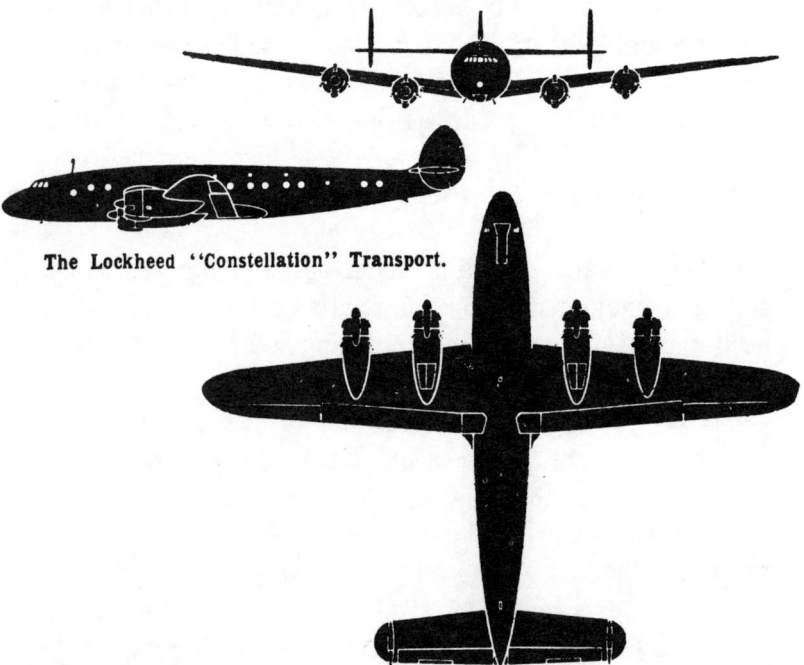

The Lockheed ''Constellation'' Transport.

76

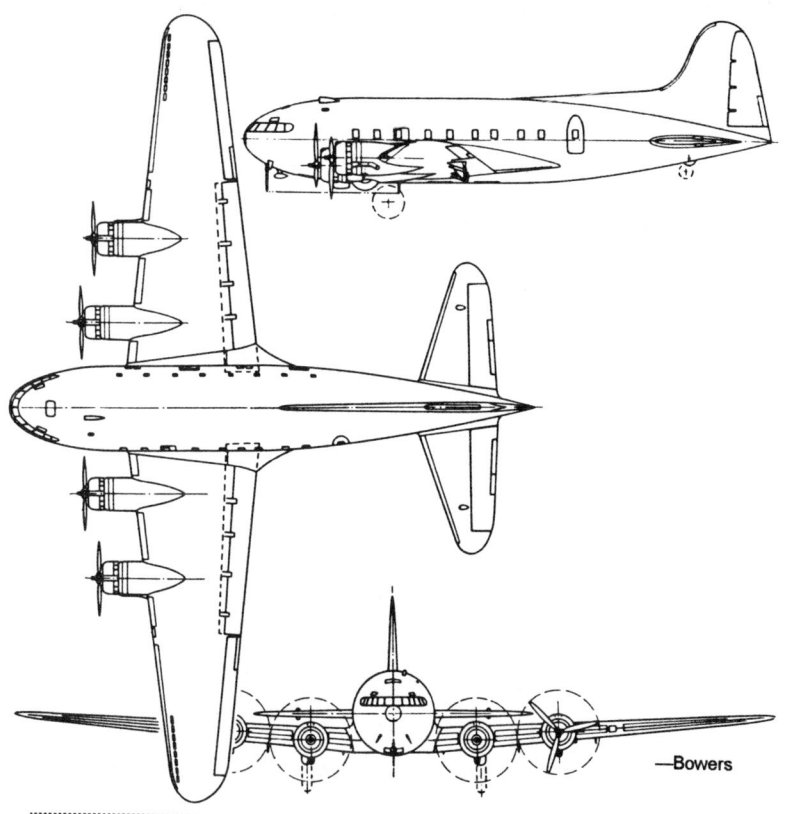

—Bowers

Only 10 of the new 33-seat 4-engine Boeing "Strato-cruiser" C-75, were built. These were for Pan American Airways and for Transcontinental and Western Air Lines (TWA). One had crashed when in test flight, The Navy commandeered them for "Executive Passengers." This C-75 was a comfortable airplane and cruised at 220 miles per hour. It had a range of 2,390 miles.

miles. It could handle 52 chaired passengers, or, in the famous butt-dead-ening bucket seats, up to 70. In 1945, there were 207 C-54's then manufactured.

Another aircraft was the Lockheed C-69 "Constellation." As for the C-69, this was intended for airline service. The C-69 had 4 engines and cruised at 255 miles per hour, had a range of about 3,500 miles and sat 46 in chairs or about 60 in the bucket seats. Regrettably, in the fall of 1945, there were only 22 C-69's in existence.

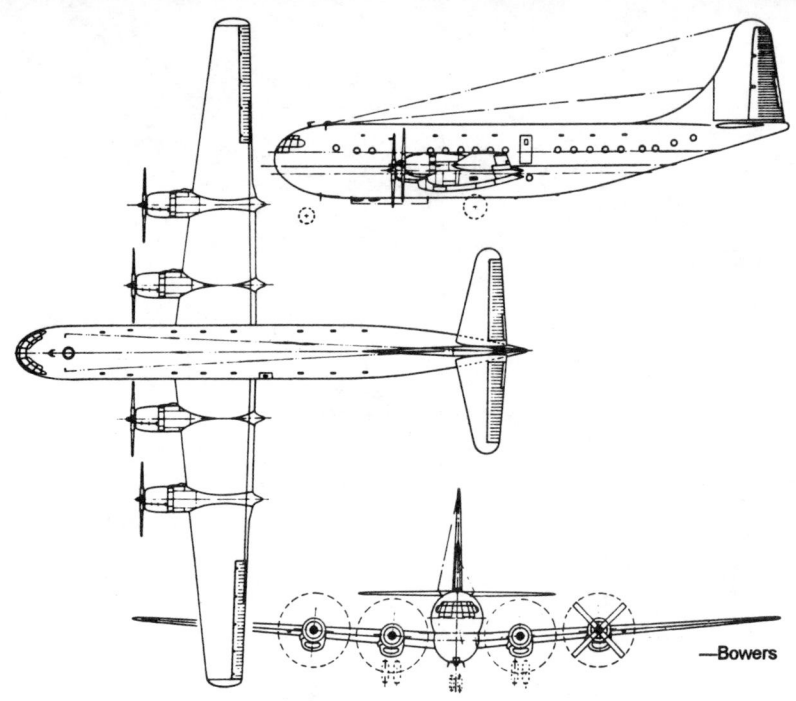

—Bowers

The best transport airplane was the 4-engine Boeing C-97 "Stratofreighter" (post-war renamed "Stratocruiser." A comfortable airplane to ride in, it was post-war used by Pan American and Northwest Orient Airlines on overseas and transcontinental flights. It was also the KC-97 air-tanker).

This was a double-deck body of the Curtis C-46 style but considerably larger. It seated between 55 and 100 airline passengers depending on configuration or 134 soldiers with packs for up to 4,300 miles. As an air-ambulance, it carried 83 litter patients. It cruised at 340 miles per hour when loaded. On a test flight from Seattle to LaGuardia Field in New York City in early 1945, the non-stop trip took only 6 hours and 3 minutes. If rushed into a troop-lift program between the United States and Japan, it could have flown non-stop from the Atlantic Coast to Seattle for fuel, then directly to Shemya. Refueling there, it could reach any point in Japan. (After the war, Northwest Orient used them between Seattle and Okinawa with the single fuel stop at Shemya.)

It would have been rare indeed to see Pan American

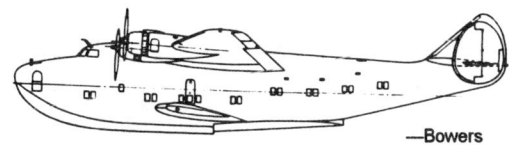

"Clipper" deluxe 4-engine flying boats carrying troops to Japan in the event of a hurry-up air-lift need. But the Boeing Model 314 "Clipper" (C-98) could carry 74 seated passengers. It was a slow, lumbering seaplane at 183 miles per hour with a range of up to 3,500 miles. Only 12 were built.

Consolidated's B-24 4-engine heavy bomber had a passenger configuration carrying only 20 people and crew of 5. It cruised at about 190 miles per hour but had a range of only 1,000 miles.

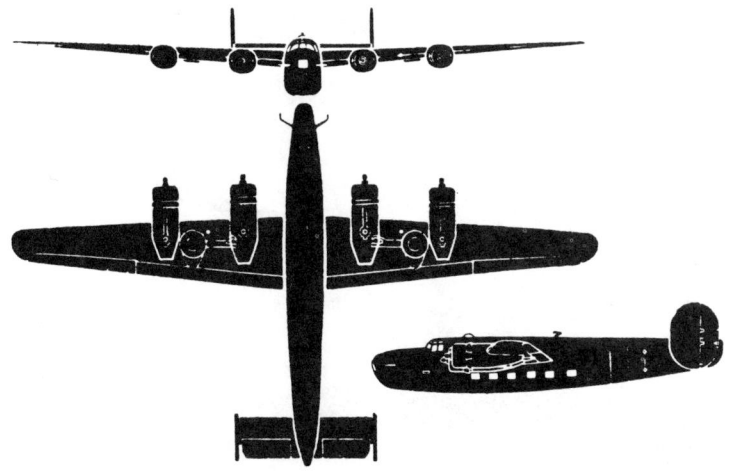

The Consolidated Vultee C-87 "Liberator" Transport.

The Curtis C-46 "Commando" twin-engine transport was designed for the very job it could now be considered – very quick deployment of paratroops. Because of the large doors (8-feet wide) on both sides of the fuselage, it was also good at hauling heavy machinery. As an example, it could carry two Jeeps. This airplane had been rushed into production from the blue-prints without testing. Because of difficulty with its fuel system, the C-46 had an embarrassing

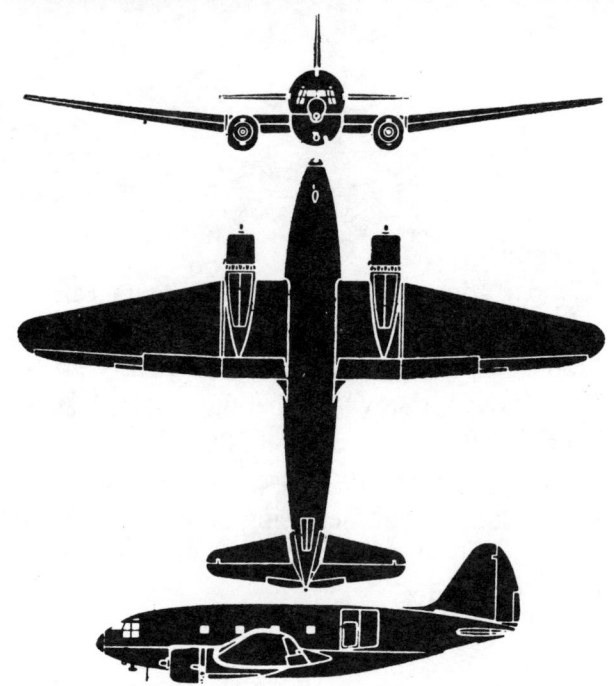

The Curtiss C-46 "Commando" Military Transport.

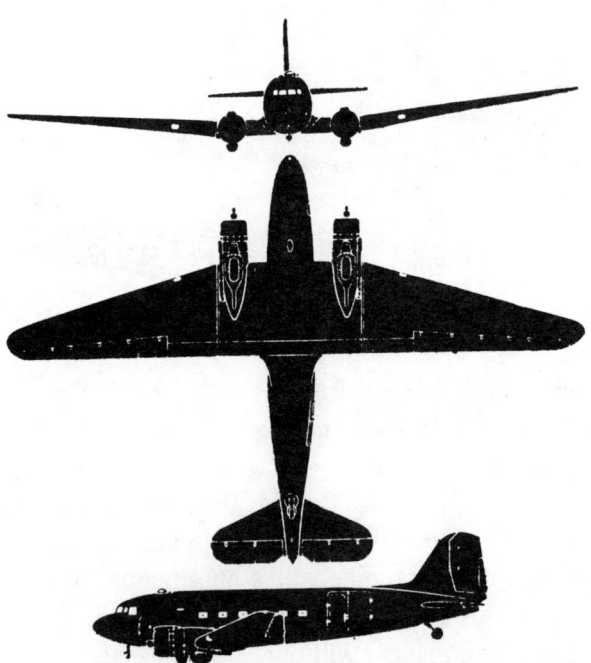

The Douglas "Skytrain" Military Transport.

habit of catching on fire. This plane had 40 folding canvas seats along the walls and room to put in 10 extra seats when required. The speed of this transport was about 250 miles per hour with a 1,600 mile range.

The C-47/C-53 Douglas twin-engine transport seated 21 passengers in airline seats or 28 fully-armed troops. The cruising speed was 170 miles per hour with a cruising distance of 1,500 miles. As was seen in some extreme evacuation conditions, the C-47 could carry up to 60 persons, without baggage, and still get off the ground. This airplane was the American "work-horse" transport of World War II and successfully served in all theaters of war.

*   *   *

Once the transport planes were loaded and ready to go, what was the best route to Japan? There would have to be "rest stops" as there were no toilet facilities to speak of on most of these airplanes. (On the C-47, as example, the built-in toilet would hold about 5 gallons – not very swift if there were 28 soldiers on long flights.)

The "passengers" would need to eat. Individual issue "K" Rations were the most practical requiring no preparation, could be issued in the face of gripes from the men, but "K" Rations would work very well.

From the Atlantic coast (Fort Bragg, as an example), the planes would go west for rest and refuel at Omaha then jump to Great Falls or to Spokane. The next leg would take the planes into either Seattle or Vancouver, B.C. Considering Boeing Field at Seattle as the "norm," as it was an established Military Air Transport System (MATS) facility, the trip from Fort Bragg was anywhere from 12 to 19 hours depending on along-the-way conditions. In event of mechanical trouble with any of the airplanes, the MATS had organized facilities at Newark, Buffalo, Detroit-Romulus, Chicago, South Bend, Omaha, Cheyenne, Great Falls, Spokane, Portland and Seattle.

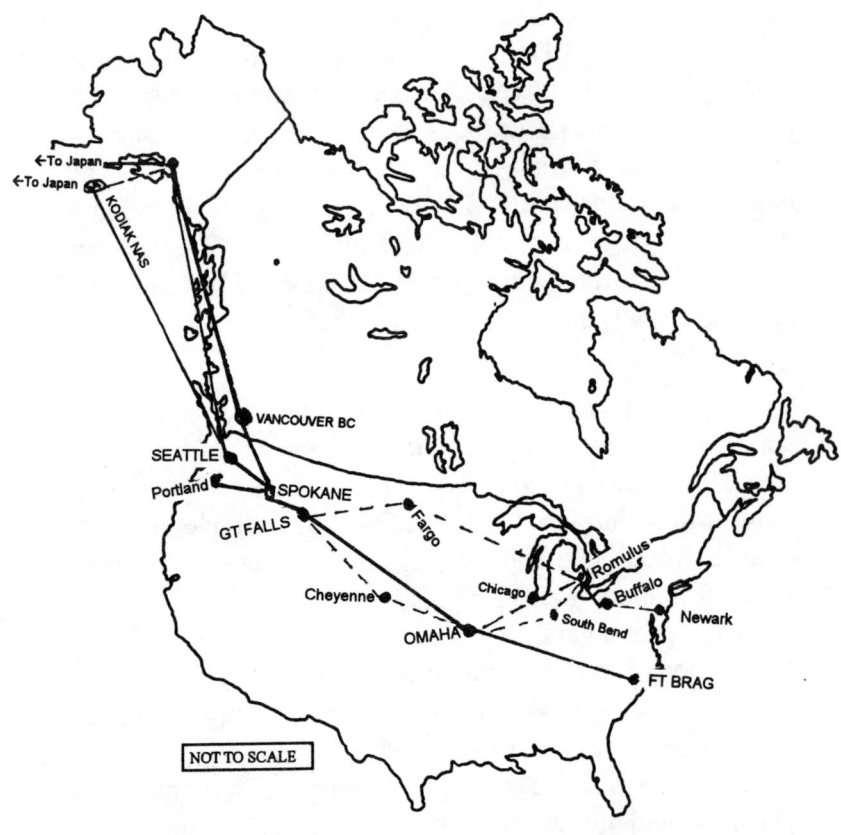

Map labels: ←To Japan, ←To Japan, KODIAK NAS, VANCOUVER BC, SEATTLE, Portland, SPOKANE, GT FALLS, Fargo, Cheyenne, Chicago, Romulus, Buffalo, South Bend, Newark, OMAHA, FT BRAG, NOT TO SCALE

The Military Air Transport Service (MATS) of the Air Force ran cross-country flights with C-47 bucket-seat airplanes seven days a week between Newark and Seattle. VIPs, Air Force Ferry Command pilots, personnel with emergency furloughs and space-available "hitchhikers" were the passengers. Sometimes, when priority air-freight was carried, passengers could be "bumped" without notice along the way. The Navy route between Seattle and Kodiak, flying C-54's, was also daily.

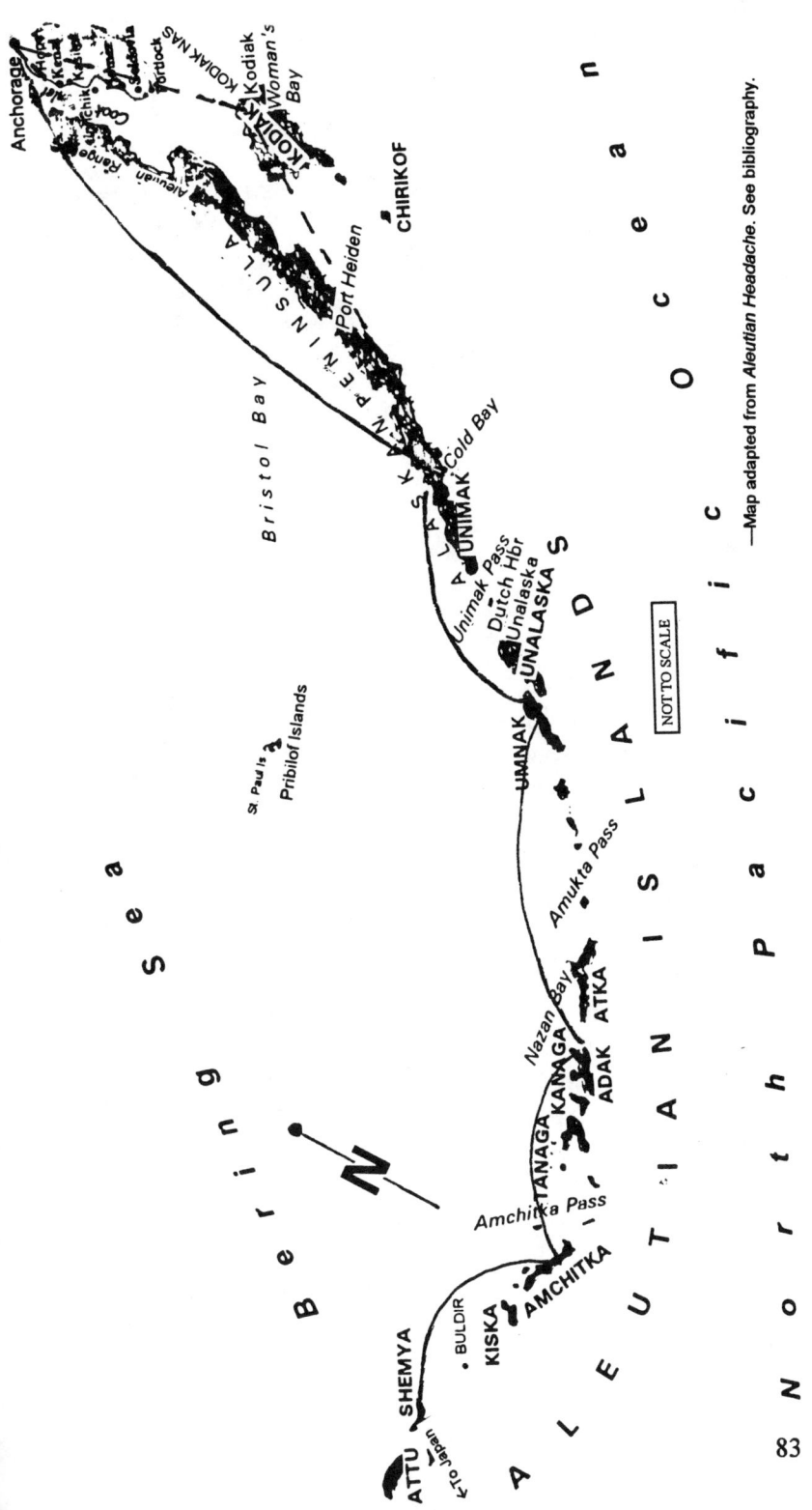

—Map adapted from *Aleutian Headache*. See bibliography.

Anchorage

Kodiak NAS
Woman's
Bay
KODIAK
CHIRIKOF

Bristol Bay

Port Heiden

A L A S K A   P E N I N S U L A

Cold Bay
UNIMAK

Unimak Pass
Dutch Hbr
Unalaska
UNALASKA

St. Paul Is.
Pribilof Islands

UMNAK

Amukta Pass

B e r i n g   S e a

Nazan Bay
ATKA
ATKA

ADAK
KANAGA

TANAGA

Amchitka Pass

AMCHITKA
KISKA
BULDIR

SHEMYA
ATTU
←To Japan

A L E U T I A N   I S L A N D S

N o r t h   P a c i f i c   O c e a n

NOT TO SCALE

N

83

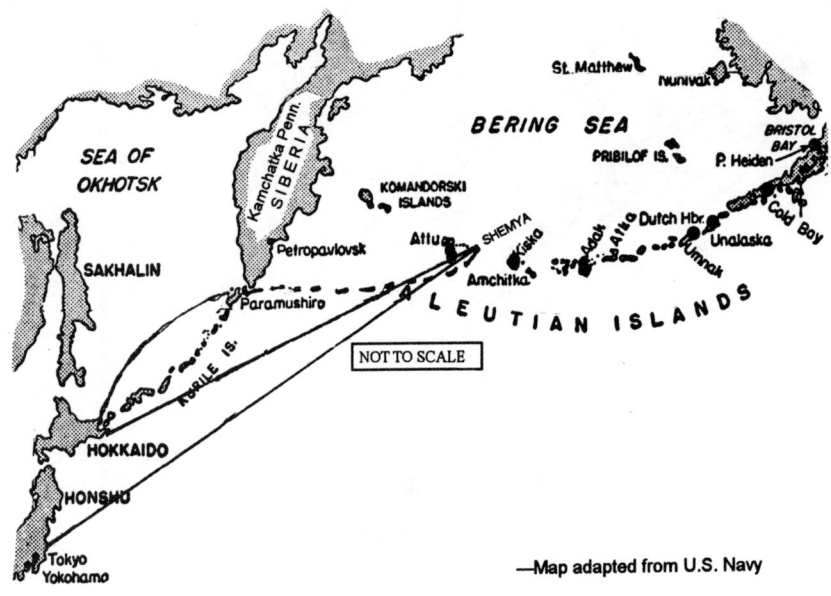

—Map adapted from U.S. Navy

From Seattle, or Vancouver B.C., the next stop was Anchorage. But the 4-engine C-54 (Navy R4D) ran a regular schedule between Sand Point NAS at Seattle to Kodiak Naval Air Station.

West from Anchorage, lay Dutch Harbor and eventually Shemya. Between Anchorage and Shemya there were airports that could be used as way stations. Some of these were Kodiak NAS, Cold Bay, Umnak, Adak and Amchitka.

The hop from the Western Aleutian Islands to Japan would depend on a couple of things. The Army Air Force and the Navy had experience with flying bombing runs from the Aleutians to Paramushiro, the northern-most Japanese base.

If, by time of Operation "Olympic," Paramushiro had been captured, it would make an excellent rest and fuel stop west of Shemya. Otherwise, it would be a long flight to Hokkaido that could be doubtful for most of the airplanes. Of course, the Boeing C-97 would have no difficulty with the range. □

Bibliography

Bowers, Peter M. *Boeing Aircraft Since 1916*. Putnam. 1966.

Davis, James Martin . *TOP SECRET; The Story of the Invasion of Japan*. Private print. 1986.

Hald, Christian P. M.D. "Atomic Bombing of Japan, Another View" in *The Daily Tidings*. Aug. 8, 1991 p.4.

Hashimoto, Mochitsura. *SUNK; The Story of the Japanese Submarine Fleet 1941-1945*. Holt. 1954.

Hoyt, Edwin P. *The Battle of Leyte Gulf: The Death Knell of the Japanese Fleet*. Weybright and Talley. 1972.

Inoguchi., Capt. R. and Cdr. Tadashi Nakajima w/Roger Pineau. *The Divine Wind, The Suicide Flyers - Japan's Kamikaze Force in WW-II*. Bantam. 1958.

Japan at War. [World War-II v.26] Time-Life Books. 1980.

McComb, Don and Fred L. Worth. *World War Super Facts*. Warner. 1983.

Morison, Samuel Eliot. *History of the United States Naval Operations in World War II*. Vol. XII, *Leyte; June 1944 - January 1945*. Atlantic. 1963.

_____. *History of the United States Naval Operations in World War II*. Vol. XIV, *Victory in the Pacific - 1945*. Holt. 1961.

_____. *History of the United States Naval Operations in World War II*. Vol. XV. *Supplement and General Index*. Holt. 1962.

Nagatsuka, Ryuji. *I Was A Kamikaze*. Macmillan. 1972

Orita, Zenji and Joseph D. Harrington. *I-Boat Captain*. Major. 1976.

Quick, John. *Dictionary of Weapons & Military Terms*. McGraw. 1973.

Reese, Lee Fleming. "Japan's Secret Revealed - She Did Have THE Bomb" in *The Military Press*. (San Diego). Jul. 1, 1989. p. 6.

Shepley, CPT James and BGEN Thomas North and LTC Paul T. Carroll, MSG Ruth Zeigler, COL H. M. Pasco. *General Marshall's Victory Report on the Winning of World War II in Europe and the Pacific*. War Dept. USA. 1945.

Taylor, Michael J. H. (Ed.) *Jane's Encyclopedia of Aviation*. Portland House. 1989.

Watts, A. J. and B. G. Gordon. *The Imperial Japanese Navy*. Doubleday. 1971.

Webber, Bert. *Aleutian Headache; Deadly World War II Battles on American Soil*. Webb Research Group. 1993.

_____. *Silent Siege-III: Japanese Attacks on North America in World War II; Ships Sunk, Air raids, Bombs Dropped, Civilians Killed*. Webb Research Group. 1992.

Wilcox, Robert K. *Japan's Secret War*. Morrow. 1985.

Index

Entries in *bold face italic* type are illustrations

EXTRA

The Weather

The Parkersburg News
A Nationally Newspaper—Leased Wire of United Press

Established 1897

Parkersburg, West Virginia, Tuesday Morning, August 14, 1945.

10 Pages. Five Cents

PEACE!
WAR ENDS!
JAPS SURRENDER!

SAN FRANCISCO, Aug. 13—(UP)—Tokyo radio reported tonight (1:49 a.m. Tuesday EWT) that an Imperial message accepting the Allied Potsdam unconditional surrender declaration would be announced shortly.

(An Office of War Information dispatch based on a Federal Communications Commission recording said flatly that the Japanese government had accepted the surrender terms.) The announcement came at 2:49 p.m. Tuesday, Tokyo time—90 hours